Building Champions

7 Success Principles for Youth Sports & the "Game of Life"

Jeff Pierce

Building Champions

7 Success Principles for Youth Sports & the "Game of Life"

Written by Jeff Pierce

ISBN: 978-0-9859200-1-2

Printed in the United States of America

WARNING – DISCLAIMER

This 2nd Edition of "Building Champions" is in dedication to my lovely wife of 32 years who recently has been diagnosed with stage 4 colon cancer.

She exemplifies the courage of a Warrior as she competes against this dangerous disease.

Her loving, caring compassion heartfelt connection to the many youth lives she has touched has also guided me to become a better person and has she been my mentor for my inspiration to help youth become all they can be.

MY LOVE FOR YOU ALWAYS HONEY!!!

Table of Contents

Foreword

This is a David and Goliath story which every one of us has, and the choice is yours to find the power of David within you.

Getting your mind to work for you rather than against you is a key ingredient to winning in sports and winning in life.

Jeff Pierce has laid out a clear step-by-step action plan to win in every aspect of your life in "Building Champions."

If you are a young athlete, read this book to give you the foundation you need to step fully into your greatness.

If you are a coach, read this book as you are in a powerful position of influence. Use this book as a tool to guide you so your influence has a positive effect on those that you coach.

If you just want to take your life into championship form in your business and family life, read this book.

"Building Champions" is an easy read with easy steps to your own championship. But, "that which is easy to do, is easy not to do". No one has ever won a championship without taking persistent clear action. Read and become inspired to take your next steps and enjoy every aspect of the journy as you go.

– *Dave Austin, international best-selling author of "Be a Beast" and 25 year mental performance coach for athletes and business executives*

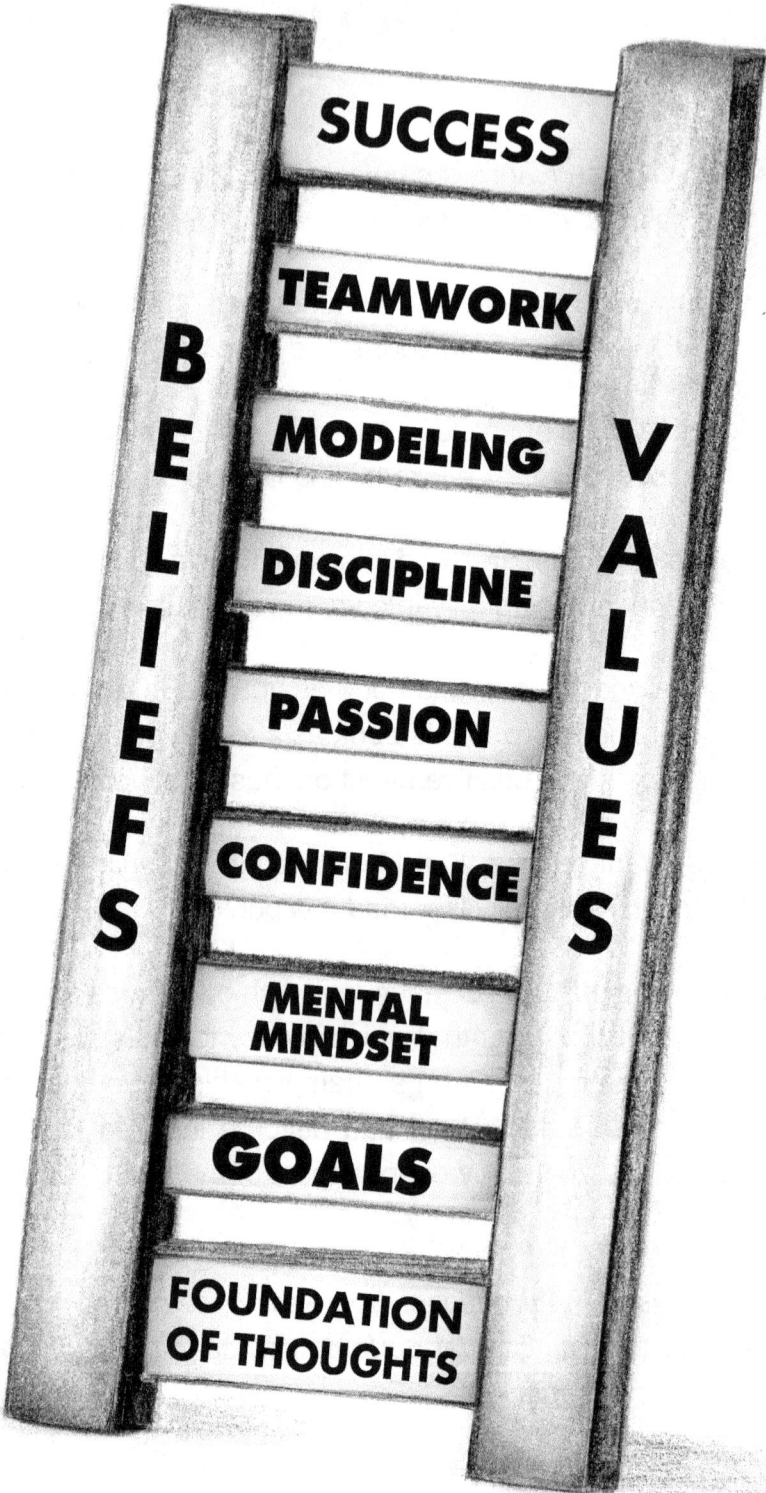

Introduction:
The Ladder Of Success
A Champion Must Climb

This book is about accomplishing goals and attaining success in life. Countless people of every age feel that success has somehow passed them by. Success is the accomplishment of reaching a Goal. What they don't realize is that goal achievement is not a chance happening. It's an intentional step-by-step process I've outlined in the **Ladder of Success**:

Every step along the ladder counts, each one bringing you closer and closer to your ultimate aim: to accomplish your desired success to become the person you choose to be. The ladder rests on a solid foundation made up of your thoughts and decisions. As you climb the ladder, you are propelled by your values and beliefs. With each step you take, you build yourself up as a champion – a champion in the game of life.

   A. The Foundation. Success starts with a person's thoughts and the decisions they make. In fact, everything in life begins with a thought. From that original thought a seed of growth develops. All of us have seeds of greatness within us, but it's the decisions we make after the thought comes into being that determine what direction the thought takes.

   B. Values and Beliefs. Everything we do in life, including each of our accomplishments, is controlled by our specific values and beliefs. In the Ladder of Success, these form

1

the handrails we hold on to as we climb to becoming that person we so desire, as well as the ladder's very support structure. Our values and beliefs give us the stability we need to reach success.

C. Goals and Dreams. The first step on the ladder is the decision that was made from the thought of what you want. More commonly, we refer to this as developing a goal. Before you can work towards anything, you need to know what you are working towards. Even though you are at the starting point, you must have the end in mind. This is your dream, which you will put in writing.

D. Mental Mindset. You need to maintain the right mental attitude to continue to the next step. The right mental mindset is a requirement for all forms of achievement. This by all means is the most vital principle of all achievement.

E. Confidence. With the wrong mental mindset you will not have the confidence to push forward with the backbone that is needed to fulfill your dreams and goals.

F. Passion. The more passion you put into whatever you're involved with, the more easily you'll create a path with less resistance.

G. Discipline. To continue heading in the direction you must go to attain any success or goal, you have to be disciplined in all you do.

H. Modeling. When you model your approach to that of someone who has previously accomplished your same goal or one similar to yours, you will have a path to duplicate.

I.   Teamwork. No one is proficient in all that needs to be done to accomplish any major goal. Therefore you must reach out and develop a team of players who have the best skills available. This creates a win-win for everyone involved.

J.   Success. You have now climbed the ladder to the top. Call it success or attainment of a specific goal. Either way, you're an achiever, a Champion in the Game of Life!

In between each rung of the ladder there is the **work** that needs to be done to be able to reach that next step. Climbing to the next step requires **action**. Combining your drive and determination to accomplish your goal with your disciplined commitment enables you to claim your "why" behind the success you're striving to achieve. Your "WHY" is the driving force to achieving any goal. The bigger your "why," the more push you have instilled in yourself to attain your success.

Building Champions: 7 Success Principles for Youth Sports and the Game of Life teaches you how to climb the Ladder of Success to win at life. Chapter 1 focuses on establishing a solid foundation through the model of youth sports. Handled correctly, youth sports is *not* about winning at all costs. It's about learning how to do your personal best and being there for the team, contributing to others for the betterment of all. This is the right approach not just in sports, but in any life endeavor.

Chapters 3 through 9 reveal the secrets to the seven success principles – the seven rungs of the Ladder of Success. Each principle – **Goals & Dreams, Mental Mindset, Confidence, Passion, Discipline, Modeling,** and **Teamwork** – is expounded upon in detail. Finally, the Epilogue ties everything together, making it crystal clear that *you* have what it takes to climb the ladder and attain the success you desire.

This book shows how to build Champions in life. Whether you're a student, a coach, a parent, a teacher, or a mentor, you can benefit from the principles taught in **Building Champions**. By the end of the book, you will be equipped with what you need to climb the Ladder of Success – or help a young person climb that ladder – and reach your goals at the top.

Let's begin by exploring the importance of a solid foundation using the common ground of youth sports.

Building

The

CHAMPION

In

YOU

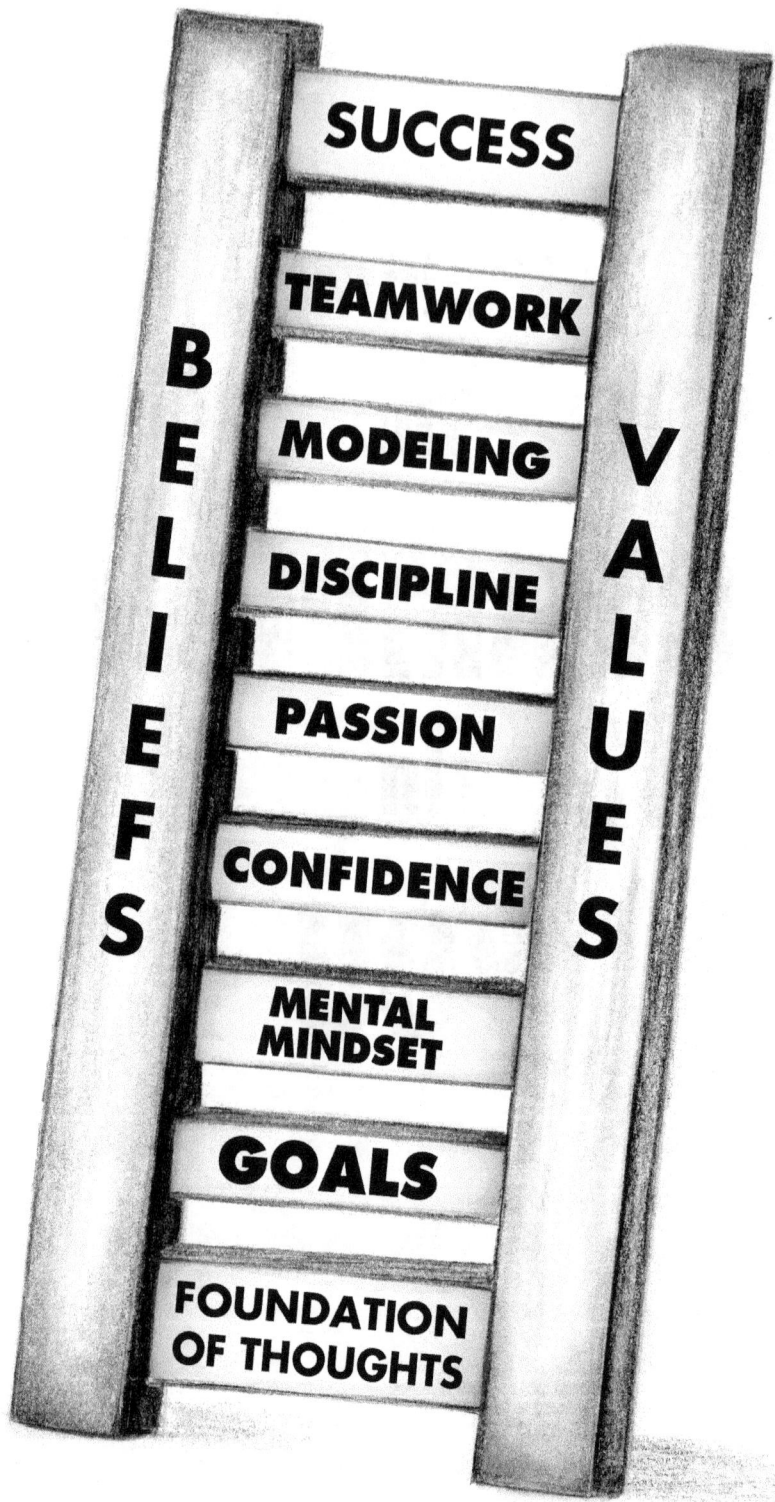

Chapter 1:
YOUTH SPORTS –
The Foundation of Their Future

What does it mean to win? What does it mean to lose? Can a winner be a loser, and is a loser ever a winner? I believe there are many possible answers to these questions and yet, when I asked an NCAA coach if a winner could be a loser, he was puzzled. He couldn't come up with an answer. There was a time when I would have had the same look and thought. If you really think about it, though, I'm sure you can remember a time when a winner let his victory overcome him. He acted immaturely, disrespected his opponent, or regarded his victory in a brash and brazen manner. I recall not long ago watching this kind of winner's actions. This behavior lost the "winner" a lot of fans, in the long run turning him into a loser. He lost respect from many loyal fans who now have a totally different outlook on this man's character. He may have been a role model in the past, but because of his immature behavior that image has been shattered. Ultimately, this winner has become a loser in many ways. A winner should be humble, never cocky or egotistical. In my view, poor behavior is a reason to classify a winner as a loser.

Now look at the opposite scenario: Can a loser be a winner? One athlete who comes to mind is Canadian Olympic hurdler Perdita Felicien, who trained for years to run in the 2004 Olympics and was favored to win. Not very far into the final race, though, she stumbled on a hurdle and fell. She lost big that day. Yet the following day while being interviewed, she said something to the effect of, "I don't know why it happened but it did, and I'm going to use it. I'm going to focus even more and work even harder for the next four years. Who knows what my path would have been had I won? Maybe it would have dulled my desire. I don't know, but I do know that now I'm hungrier than ever. I'll be back even stronger." Do you think that she gained respect from hundreds if not thousands of people from her response to losing? In the end she won in much greater ways than getting a medal. How she took a defeat and used it is motivation to me, an inspiration in itself.

Here's another example. Would you say that Michael Vick, quarterback for the Philadelphia Eagles, can be classified a winner after losing millions of dollars as well as the respect of many? After his huge error in judgment and time spent in jail, he's come back and rebuilt his sports career. To me, this is the sign of a real winner. He is a good example of how someone can lose badly but then turn around and apply the **7 Success Principles**, discussed in detail in the following pages, to rebuild not only his career but his life.

Winners and losers can be described in many ways, so being a winner or loser is simply a matter of perception. It's really about the meaning that we give to these words. I'd say this is true about many things, if not everything, in our lives. If you watched your favorite team lose in the Super Bowl with a score of 31-7, would you have a different feeling, perception or outlook than if your team had won 31-7? It's safe to say that if you asked a fan from each team what their view of the game was, they would have different responses and different outlooks on the exact same game.

In reality, our lives are based on perception, which is the way we look at what is going on around us. It's another word for the view from the "rose-colored glasses" we are wearing. If you are having a bad day, is there a chance you'd find something good about it if you really tried? If you look at what at first you think is bad, could you actually see the possibility of something positive or some good coming from the experience? Many times in life we look at a situation as being a disastrous event or perhaps the end of the world when in fact it could be a motivating factor we can use to propel us to a path of excellence. Couldn't this also be true about losing a game, a match or any competition?

"The difference between the impossible and the possible lies in a man's determination."
– Tommy Lasorda

It's been said that Thomas Edison had a thousand failures before inventing the light bulb. Henry Ford went bankrupt before developing the first automobile. These great inventors and entrepreneurs would not have achieved their accomplishments had they simply given up. It was their desire, dedication, drive, determination and discipline that gave them the strength to continue their journey and to never give in to the doubts of the people around them. We need to be grateful for the people who came before us who have given us the luxuries we are blessed with. Their belief in themselves has given us plenty to be thankful for. By looking back at how successful people have succeeded you can see the traits and behaviors of what it takes to be a success in all you do.

At some point, all of us have classified ourselves as losers. Of course, this isn't the case, but it is our perception. Too often we allow this misperception to hold us back or give us a sense of failure. Why do most people simply settle? It's much better to take those times of failure and use them to our advantage. The best way to react to such situations is to "*attack them*," to take the challenge and overcome the obstacles. To reach the highest level that you are capable of. At some point, you *will* reach the pinnacle of your success. No, you don't have to be the ultimate gold medal winner. You could win the bronze and take something from the experience, use what you have learned, and apply those skills and tools to create success in the future and determine your destiny. Keep in mind a Bronze Medal Olympic athlete became a Bronze medal winner by being victorious over hundreds if not thousands of competitors. Just because on that specific day or event there where two people better does NOT mean that he or she isn't a true champion. That could be their ultimate success. Was it their perspective that they succeeded? Don't let someone else determine or justify your success. What you are about to read in the next pages will serve as your stepping stones to making small daily adjustments to achieve the goals, dreams, and desires of your choice.

A winner is only a winner based on the picture you're painting, and likewise with a loser. The only true loser is the person who gives up without learning something important, or without taking the lesson learned and moving forward. A so-called loser is not a loser at all if he takes his loss and uses it as a learning experience to propel himself to his ultimate destiny.

As a coach, businessman, father, and student of life, I've deciphered what principles are needed to attain success in sports and in life in general. My goal with this book is to pass on my findings through a simple set of small, manageable daily actions for youth and adults to achieve whatever they truly set their minds to. The principles presented in the following pages can be used by youth in sports and then expanded further to apply to all areas of life. My goal is to teach young people that these same principles are important when their sports days are over.

If you are to live fully, no matter what your age you must never give up on learning. When I was younger I did not enjoy reading. Actually, I despised it to the bone. But once I started reading on a regular basis, I can honestly say that I was amazed. I had never ever imagined I could learn so much. Reading about and studying successful people gave me a different perspective. What once seemed a waste of time turned into some of the most enlightening moments of my life. To read and understand more of how the brain works and how we all let ourselves be controlled by our subconscious has really inspired me to find solutions. Through this book, I hope to pass along inspiration and empowerment to youth and adults to live abundantly in every area of their choosing.

To give you a better understanding of me and my journey, let me tell you a little about myself. I was born in Binghamton, NY in the mid 1950s to lower middle class parents. At the age of five, I was enrolled in a special class to help me learn how to speak better as I had a speech impediment. This continued for 3 years in 3 different schools. I was also blessed at the age of 6 to begin to wear glasses, not very common back at that time. Picture this, a skinny kid that can't talk with the funny looking glasses, well that was me. I was fighting adversity from a very young age.

Then during my fourth or fifth grade, my father up and walked out and left my mother with four kids, no job and no money left in the bank. During the few months he was gone it certainly affected me as when he returned after a few weeks he was immediately admitted to the hospital for a mental evaluation. Fortunately, I don't remember how long this issue disrupted my life but it did have a lasting effect.

When he was finally released from the hospital he was able to regain employment and we seemed to be getting back to normal, normal as I knew it at that age, even though I had taken *a bull whip to the backside as a punishment.* Somehow my father was then promoted into a management training program. This eventually led to me going to ten schools during my 13 years of formal education. I was always that tall skinny new kid on the block with funny looking glasses. I was that kid that everyone picked on. I was made aware of bullying before it was even called "bullying". More than once I got knocked out while playing around when my so called "friends" would go get the boxing gloves. I was always the test opponent to anybody that came around.

During my high school years I participated in soccer and wrestling. My days playing soccer were extremely limited, as I didn't have the coordination or skills to even play second string. *I was the official benchwarmer!!!* I was the one that everyone laughed at and picked on when I couldn't perform a specific drill, or missed a pass. Wrestling was no different, but fortunately, my first coach was one that never let anyone get down on themselves because of their lack of ability and he pushed everyone to just do their best. For me that paid off, as in my third year of wrestling we had moved to Corning-Painted Post, NY and due to a lack of participants I was placed on varsity my junior year. It certainly wasn't because of my ability. I was the only one available for the weight class. You see I didn't even win 25% of my matches, heck, maybe not even 10%.

As I explain my "story" rest assured you will find the purpose to why I tell you these items as you make your way through the book. It's not for you to feel sorry for me as I can say all these things from my past happen "for" me not "to" me.

I did learn some valuable life lessons when we lived in Painted Post. The morning of the last day of my sophomore year at 2:00 AM we were awakened by our neighbors and told to get out fast as the dike broke up the river and we needed to get out fast due to the ensuing surge of water if we were to survive. Shortly after 2:00 AM I carried my then 8 year old sister out on my shoulders in waist deep water.

Having only lived in the area for 3 months we knew very few people. We ended up living with 32 people in one house with no electric for 6 days before we could get out of town and head to our relatives. At the age of 16, I was forced to learn the building trade as my father also lost the lumber yard he managed due to the flood. That whole summer was spent sleeping on the plywood floors and eating at rescue centers while we rebuilt our home. My father was too proud to take government housing. I can now thank him for that as it certainly helped me grow substantially that summer.

In my senior year, at yet another school district, Watertown, NY, I was again the official benchwarmer on the soccer team. However, part way through the soccer season during a conversation with some of the soccer players I let out that I would be going out for the wrestling team. Well, another round of being bullied was about to begin. Little did I know but the weight that I wrestled my junior year was taken by a fellow soccer teammate that really enjoyed pushing me around and making fun of me. Needless to say, he made it very clear that he would be taking me out one way or another as there was no way I would be taking his spot on the wrestling team. So for about 3 more weeks it was like a living hell from this kid.

Well, the first day of wrestling practice was to begin and maybe it was a blessing in disguise as in gym class I took a basketball into the end of my fingers and dislocated a knuckle which kept me from wrestling and having to deal with my soccer bully teammate. Thinking back on it; that basketball may have saved my life.

Just prior to graduating from high school, my parents were forced to respond to yet another move request; this time to Bangor, Maine. Needless to say when they went to look at the area, the site where my Dad's new company building would be built was flooded. In short my mother had one reply, "We are not moving into another flood area, if we move anyplace we're moving back home to the Southern Tier of NY."

Well, this demoralized my Dad to take a demotion and get back into sales. Within two months he was mentally unstable again and tried to commit suicide. My life was going to head back through hell once again. The short version is that I was then the only man in the house with an income at age 18 and was forced to help my Mom raise my two younger sisters as my parents divorced. I found out really fast the struggles to survive. I even at times had to throw my own father out of the house when he would come for visitation with my sisters as he threatened to kill my mother and sisters.

Since coming back home to Endicott, NY after High School I worked a few years at a local lumber yard and was quickly promoted to outside contractor sales, which meant my father was now my competition. Within a few years to get away from the battle with my own father I started a design-build construction company at the age of 23. I eventually was one of the top 5 builders in the area. During this time I got married to my wonderful wife and became an instant Dad to three step-children.

Then, the recession set in during the early 1990's taking 6500 jobs from our area; and there was only one new construction building permit issued that year. Within six months my attorney recommended I close the doors, claim bankruptcy, and look for something else. This all happening at a time when we found out that after two miscarriages and 14 years spread from my youngest step daughter we were going to have my own biological son. The birth of my son is the only thing that helped me remain somewhat mentally stable. However, the responsibility to be able to support four children, keep a roof over our heads and move forward was extremely stressful and demoralizing as I felt that I had let them all down. I had to fight hard not to fall into the same trap that I saw my father fall into and let the mental frustration win a victory over me like it did my Dad.

During this time I had started a new job in commercial construction and was on the road traveling. This became a challenge for my wife and my youngest son. During our wait for his Pinewood Derby Cub Scout races at the age of seven we saw what they call in our area "Microds" which are basically go-carts. I was surprised my son didn't show any interest in them and asked him why, the reply was devastating *"You'd never let me have one and we don't have money for it anyway."* You can imagine how demoralizing that was to a Dad. Well, that was when I realized I needed to find a way. I had no idea how I was going to get a car but with much soul searching, I felt that I needed to get him a car for 2 reasons:

1. So we could spend family time together both at the track but also in working on the car with my son.
2. To help my son learn RESPECT. Respect for himself, respect for others, respect for his car and others cars.

Well, this was a turning point in my understanding the power of sports. Even though I had coached my step-son and my own biological son for years in travel soccer, I realized over the next 5-6 years of racing that the power of focus is so important. I then started to watch sports at every level in a different way. From youth sports, to professional sports and mostly the Olympics, it was apparent that the successful athletes were doing things that others weren't. I then started researching and looking for the common denominators between success in sports and success in business. My findings are what you will find within "Building Champions".

During this time our son was going from "Microds" (go-carts) to racing with adults in Legends cars (which run at close to

100mph) at the age of 13. This is will be a more in depth discussion later when we talk about confidence. I was also helping coach Pee Wee wrestling that our grandson participated in. This was another eye opening experience from youth sports.

Due to a few situations, things then began to take a very different direction in my life. It was back in March of 2006 a few days after my 50th birthday.

Back On the Mat

What was I getting myself into? Here I stood on the side of a wrestling mat waiting for my match to begin. This crazy thought running through my head "What is this skinny 50 year old man who hasn't wrestled in 33 years thinking?"

In preparation for this day, I had spent two months working on my cardio and mental preparation for what was before me. I had to have a "Game plan." I thought—I had to work on the basics. I knew that if I was to have any chance, I had to be mentally prepared as well as I had to know I wasn't going to die of a heart attack while on the mat.

So to get started, I stepped foot into a Team Worldwide Wrestling Club practice. It was a day of enlightenment as I was not the only *crazy old man* there. Here stood another gentleman that gave me some reassurance that I hadn't totally lost my mind. However, the next morning that all seemed to change as I could barely get out of bed. So, as I lied there, the reason for this crazy idea then re-emerged. You see the reason for doing this was I had unfinished business. In my senior year in high school I had an accident on the basketball court in gym class that prevented me from wrestling. How could I, a wrestler, let basketball take that away? Well it had worn on me for years and now that I was helping coach pee wee kids getting into the sport of wrestling I had to show them that if "I could do it, they could do it." And yet one of the most important reasons for doing this was I was fed up with seeing and hearing how coaches are treating our youth. My own son and many of his buddies had quit playing sports their senior year in high school because they had become upset with how the coaches had their favorites and would treat the rest of the kids on the team with little or no respect. By this time my son had spent years running his Legends race car at close to 100mph with adults and fully understood the meaning of respect not just for himself, but for others in the sport. So for him, it was extremely frustrating that these high school coaches didn't respect him and his buddies thus the kids dropped out of sports. It came to a climax when at one of our Pee Wee wrestling tournaments, a coach went on and on about how his kids didn't listen to him. When I questioned him about when was the last time he stepped on to a mat and faced what they have to face, his response was that he never wrestled. How could this coach become so upset with these young first time wrestlers for not giving him the results that *he* expected when he had never even wrestled?

Just 2 weeks prior to this I had been doing some research to find some tournaments for our team and I had run across an Old-Timers Tournament. I had this crazy thought how cool would that be to wrestle in something like this. Needless to say, all those times came back to me of lying there on my back getting pinned time and time again. Then of course, everybody I had mentioned it to said I would be crazy to think of something like this at close to fifty years old.

Now that this other coach was demeaning these young athletes, I told him that I had just found something that he should participate in that would help him understand what his young athletes were facing. Needless to say I was told "You're Crazy!" Well, he wasn't the first one that told me that, so I told him I'd be looking for him that day. If he was really serious about helping his athletes, he would be willing to put himself in the same shoes.

Envision this… Here is this skinny 50 year old that had opened his mouth and now had to find a way to be prepared for the challenge before me. In preparation for that day I had to have enough **Self-Confidence** to get myself in shape so that I could step on the mat to compete and know that they wouldn't have to carry me off on a stretcher. In addition, at that age it took a lot of **Discipline** to dedicate the time needed and overcome the pain of getting into shape to be able to compete. Lastly, I have always had **Passion** for the sport as I know that it has provided me fundamentals and principles that I have used in business and the "Game of Life."

I believe wrestling is a great avenue for teaching success principles to youths.

So after hearing about this Old Timers Tournament I set a **Goal** that I would wrestle before I turned fifty. Unfortunately, due to bad timing I wasn't able to wrestle in a tournament before my 50th birthday, but I was able to do so the following weekend. Believe me, when I stepped on the mat I really had to work on my **Mental Mindset – "The Inner Game**." At that moment, I fully realized just how much you can learn from sports.

> *"It's lack of faith that makes a person afraid of meeting challenges, and I believed in myself"."*
> **Muhammed Ali**

So, as I warmed up on the edge of the mat waiting for my match on this day in March, 2006, it certainly was a lonely feeling thinking that here I am at 50 yrs. old with all these younger guys, most in better physical shape then myself, that one of these guys would soon be my nemesis. Well, as my luck would have it, as time drew closer by process of elimination, I pretty much determined who my opponent was going to be. Wouldn't you know it, just like 3 years in high school I was going to be the underdog before I even stepped foot on that mat. Here stands this young man with arms and legs twice the size of mine and I would guess probably in his mid 20's, but I was hoping he was really in his 30's and extremely muscle bound. Anything I could do to sway any small advantage my way I was fighting to do so. Then, to add insult to injury, my then 9 yr old grandson comes up and says, "Grandpa, are you really wrestling that really big guy? *He's HUGE!*" I guess you can tell what that did to my mental mindset! I knew I had to really dig deep and I mean really, really deep. It was at this point that I had to make this a turning point in my life; that was if I was to live!!! You see, I had to fight back the thoughts of all the times in high school that came back to me, where I was laying there looking up at the lights and fighting not to get pinned. So you ask, "Why would you look to wrestle again at 50? You OLD MAN!!! Are you an Idiot?"—I guess so! Call it whatever you want but I had many feelings about it. One, if I was going to send these young, inexperienced kids out to step on a mat against other kids, then I should be willing to do it myself. Wrestling to me is the biggest character building high school sport there is. I know it changed my life back in the day and it would change it further this day also.

As I ran out to the center circle it was me and him. This skinny 50 yr old against this 28 yr old fit Marine home on leave. You could say I was physically overmatched. With a huge wave of mixed emotions running through me I knew I had worked hard for 2 months, I had mentally prepared myself for my competition but little did I know this would be my competition. It was all about to begin, a rematch of "*David versus Goliath*". A point in my life when I was totally out of my comfort zone.

As the match progressed, I continued to battle this *GIANT* sized young man. Yes, we may have weighed the same, but I was 5-6 inches taller than him, however he was built much better than this skinny old man. He no doubt tossed weights like me around like sacks of potatoes in the gym.

I survived the first period and realized that I was in a battle that I'm sure everyone in the crowd originally thought was going to be about a 10 second match. I'm sure people thought I'd be stomped on like an ant being stepped on by a human; that I'd be crushed in no time.

The second period was very much like the first period, a see-saw battle back and forth and no one really gained any large advantage over the other. The Old Man was holding his own.

Well, I did what I had to do, did I win the match? You bet I did. I didn't win on the score board, but I won in the "Game of Life". I really don't know the final score as I never looked at the scoreboard but I was told it was 2-1. To me it was one of the largest victories in my life. It has been a catalyst for most of what I do now.

In the end I know the only reason I didn't get carried off on a stretcher, like a gentleman in the match before me, was because I had worked hard telling myself that I HAD to get that feeling back so I could continue to help these young first time wrestlers face the same fears that I faced as I looked across that circle. I had to have full faith and confidence that I had worked hard on my cardio and mental mindset to not let anything, *including Goliath's size*, disrupt me from going out and proving that us adults, parents and coaches alike, we must let the kids enjoy the sport and have fun but instill valuable principles to them along the journey. It's the values and principles that youth learn from the sport that help them become "Champions" later on in life no matter what they do.

A switch clicked in my mind that day and I understood the common denominator of what I was doing and how it related to life outside of sports. I now look back and see how these five success principles of **Confidence, Passion, Discipline, Goals, and Mental Mindset** were critical for my survival on the mat that day.

If you analyze my story I'm sure you could imagine just like everybody else we all have stories of our life. What's important is not to live in your story but to *learn* from it. The understanding that we all need to have is it's the past story, It's now time to forget those thoughts of how your story made you feel, it's time to be focused on your thoughts at this moment and to make the best of the present moment in time. Keep in mind that your past does not represent your future if you're are willing to create a new journey. On this new journey we need to start off by building a strong foundation of new thoughts, values and beliefs.

So from what I have learned, studied personally, experienced and of coaching youth athletes, I've developed success principles to provide basic tools for today's youth and adults to apply not only in sports but also in the "Game of Life". These principles are important not only to youth sports; they are also very valuable to each and every one of us as we continue to grow, regardless of our present age or stage. It is one of our human needs to grow at every point in our lives, whether we are involved in youth sports or we're a 50-year-old stepping back into the game.

"The difference between a successful person and others is not a lack of strength, not a lack of knowledge, but rather a lack of will"

– Vince Lombardi

Look at the winners of the Super Bowl, the World Series, and the Olympics. Do they stop and quit once they have won at the highest level? NO! The entire team doesn't retire once they get that Super Bowl ring. They now have a taste of the ultimate victory, and this propels them to strive to repeat that win, or to develop other goals they can reach out to accomplish. So getting to the top is not where the winners stop; they just keep marching on and striving to continue to the next challenge.

In real life outside of sports, what would have happened if Sam Walton (patriarch of the Walton family, owners of Walmart and Sam's Club) had just stopped growing once he made his first million? He has gone on and grown the business into the largest retail company in the nation and has changed the retail shopping market all across the United States. So the philosophy to continue to grow and learn applies in the real, everyday world as well as in sports. I believe the skills and tools that anyone can learn from sports will catapult them into their achievements in real life.

The *7 Success Principles* that you will learn about are *Goals and Dreams, Mental Mindset, Confidence, Passion, Discipline, Modeling, and Teamwork.* These are principles that upon my reading, my research, and my own life experiences, I have found to be crucial to growth, reaching for the stars, and creating your destiny.

There are two people whom I specifically owe so much to, the first being Napoleon Hill, author of "Think and Grow Rich." The other person is, in my eyes, the ultimate life success coach, Anthony Robbins. Mr. Robbins has a very special ability to analyze a person, and he draws from them their inner feelings to give them the inspiration and tools to create astounding life changes. I urge each and every one of you to read any or all of his books or go to one of his seminars. You will find him to be a person full of more **Passion** than most people have. Both of these men are truly winners in my eyes.

An extremely important part of achievement is to have a powerful and emotionally driven WHY! This "Why" is your reason for why you need to accomplish any Goal or Dream. The bigger the "Why" the easier it will be to work on the action needed to reach your Goal and create your Destiny.

So let's get started on becoming a winner. Not just a winner on the field, on the mat, on the court, in the pool, on the track, or at any other sport facility, but a winner in the "GAME OF LIFE!"

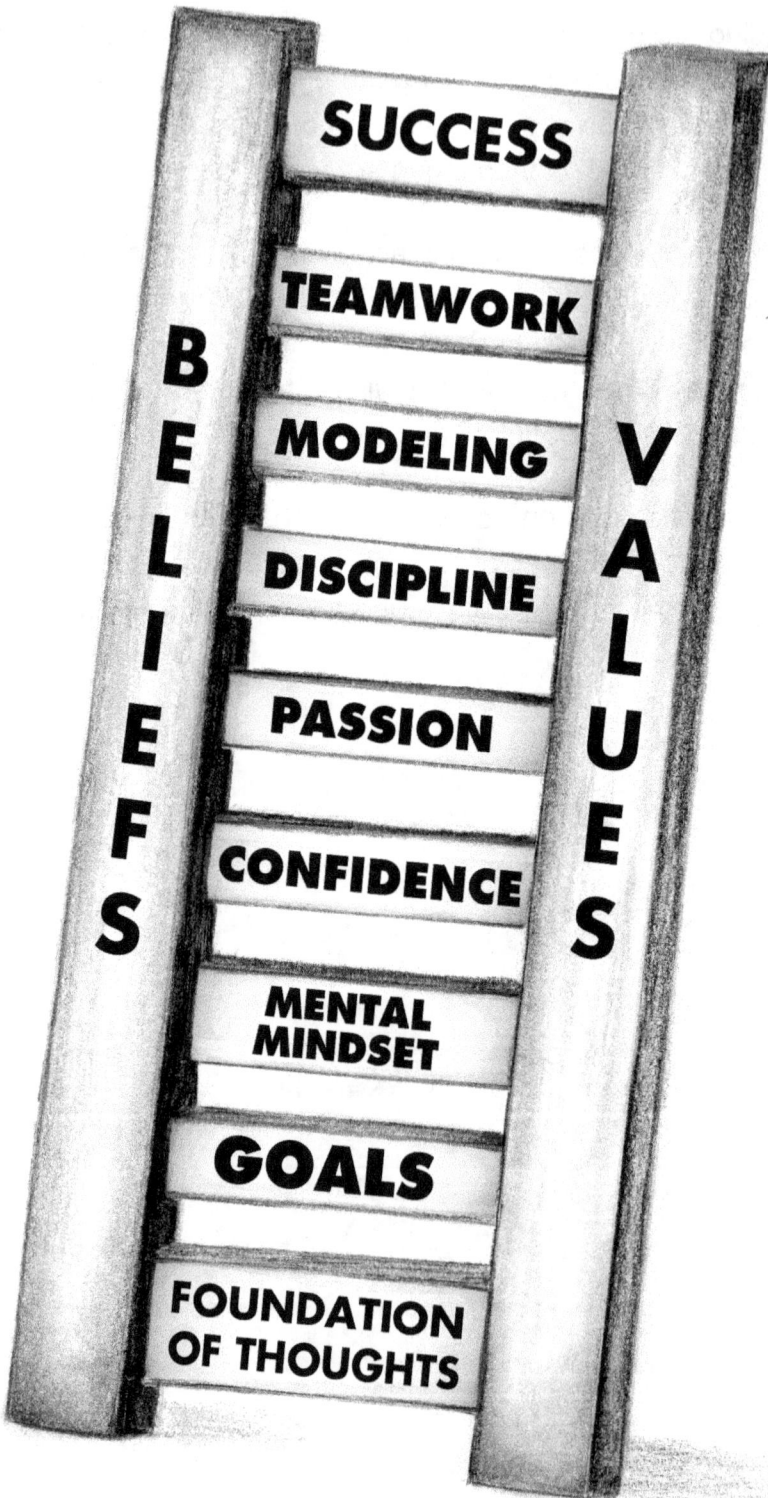

Chapter 2:
VALUES & BELIEFS –
The Guiderails

For every ladder to be strong enough to climb up it must have two stable strong side guide rails. This same aspect applies to our life, the guiderails should be the values that we live by and the beliefs that we have about ourselves.

When you have a ladder that does not have adequate guiderails the ladder will break or bust apart when you attempt to climb it. Metaphorically, it is the same as a human's life. If your values do not align with your desired outcome of who would like to *become, do, or have* then there will be a tremendous challenge to achieve your desired success and there is a very good chance something will fall apart in the process.

Another aspect that works in unison with your values is your beliefs in and about yourself. This may sound somewhat basic and simple, however, I'm sure that at some point you have noticed or could look back at an event or time in your life that you realized you didn't succeed partly in fact because you really down deep in your heart you didn't think you could or didn't think you were worthy of it.

In the last chapter I told you my story in a fair amount of detail. I did this for a reason as it's during those times of my past I was living in the wrong set of values. Now I don't mean to take anything away from my parents at all.

I love both my parents. It's the situations that I was forced to live through that I really want to talk about now as they are the conditions that I, like most people, think that that's life and we are just forced to deal with it. Well there is a lot more to it than that.

You see during my school years when I was that skinny kid with big rimmed glasses what do you my belief of myself was when I was being bullied and beat on? What values do you think I was living my life by? My life for me was painful and humiliating however, I kept that bundled up inside of me as I didn't know any better. When my Dad up and walked out I was lost and didn't feel I was loved at all. So I couldn't value the power of love in relationships, I don't believe at that time I had any sense of security. These feelings or values that weren't present in my life kept me from having any belief or confidence in myself. I certainly couldn't value things like *acceptance, affection, compassion, connection, dependability, devotion, direction, friendships, love, joy, leadership, passion, motivation, pride, teamwork, or even self-respect.* You see I wasn't living a life of fun and laughter, love, joy and happiness. Even my days playing sports I always felt lost and at the back of the pack, the odd ball.

Again I don't tell you this for you to feel sorry for me as God knows there are millions of youth that had it a lot worst then I did but I tell you this as an example of showing that it's times in our youthful years that can set a blueprint with-in our subconscious mind of what is reality when in fact it is not reality at all. It's just the perspective at that time as that is all that we know. It wasn't until I started to dive into reading and going to personal development events that I started to realize that

I was just living a "story" of my past. As Tony Robbins states "you need to get out of your story". This all really came to my understanding after my wrestling match at 50. You see as I said earlier that's when the light came on. How could I just live through the rematch of "David vs Goliath" but yet my first marriage failed, I had to claim business bankruptcy? The journey of personal analysis and growth really began at that time. I really started to analysis myself as a human *being*. Not as a human *doing*, you see that was what I was, I was doing, I was surviving and living by what others thought of me. That is so true for so many people. We let others tell us what we can do and what we can't do. Who we are and who we are not.

As you continue to read keep in mind if you are an adult or a coach this is not only insights for your young athlete, but also for any other youth and yourself.

It's time to set down and have serious conversation with yourself and really figure out WHO YOU ARE!!! There comes a time to walk the talk, of what values and beliefs you need to be living to be the person you want to be. To do what you want to do in your life, and to have what you want to have in life. It's YOUR VALUES and BELIEFS that shape who you are. Are you living by the values and beliefs that you really have down deep within yourself?? What are the values you are living by vs what are the values you should, better yet, MUST be living by to be that person you truly want to be? Do you have a strong enough belief system within yourself to be that person??

Now the last paragraph hopefully got you to take a minute to do a little thinking, if not, I recommend you go back and reread it and answer those questions. This is where I found the most growth in moving out of my past story, naturally I had put some of my past deep in my memory banks, however, that only partially solves the problem temporarily as those feelings and beliefs are programmed into your sub-conscious mind so you need to work on how you are going to reprogram that computer between your two ears.

This reprogramming has to start with the first step being self-analysis. You can't fix what you don't know is broken. Now I'm not saying you are broken as nobody is ever broken we are just in need of maintenance. It's like a car that had a set of tires put on it and 2-3 years later they have no more tread on them and they are in need of replacement. Well we are the same way, we are no doubt of replacing some of the old values that we came to inherit or ended up making a habit of living by.

If you are serious about moving to the next level in your sport, your job, your family life or even your finances you must be aware that there very well could be something you need to change to be able to get to that next level. Could it be that you need to value your time more, or do you need to value love more, or could it be you need to be more courageous??

If you need to be a better athlete you must be doing more than your competition, This could be starting your practice earlier, it could mean staying later, it could be doing an extra weight training program totally on your own, These are all items that mean that you need to value time maybe more that you do now. It could also mean that you need to be more committed and place more value on your health. This means maybe being more committed to eating healthier or getting more sleep so your mind is well rested for peak performance, or simply do you need to have a clearer understanding and value of your own worthiness? This can be a very huge obstacle to overcome for some people. Some people just don't feel they are deserving.

This feeling of not being worthy comes mostly from a lack of belief in themselves, A low self-esteem and a lack of self-confidence of what they are capable of if only they really put 100% effort into the desired goal. If you are one of those people that fights being worthy of obtaining or having anything maybe it's time to drop the *story* and live into your worthiness as we are all unique and we are all on this earth for a reason. Don't let someone else tell you or even try to insinuate that you're not good enough. If we all fall into this perspective of living our life by what someone thought, where would this world be? Would we have the growth and the technology that we do now? Would there be cell phones, computers, tablets, Apple, or whatever the next big thing is? Would there be professional sports if all youth and college athletes fell into the belief that they were just average? Or is it those that were once average are the ones that put in the extra work to find what it takes from within themselves and the belief that they must have about themselves to be able to get to the next level? So I ask if you have taken the time to start your journey by sitting down and being honest with yourself, what values are you living by and what beliefs do you have that may be stopping you when you are only that *3 feet from gold*? Don't ever settle, keep seeing and believing along the journey.

Hopefully, this chapter has given you some insight to see that everyone's life is shaped basically by what values you are living your life by everyday and then what are your beliefs of what you are capable of. Your success is not determined by your limitations as right next to whatever you think that limitation may be there is an opportunity. So I urge you do not let your setbacks hold you back. Don't ever settle.

"One of the most common causes of failure is the habit of quitting when one is overtaken by temporary defeat"

Napolean Hill excerpt from "Think and Grow Rich"

If we look at the time when nobody thought anyone could run faster than the 4 minute mile nobody would have ever imagined that once it was accomplished that it would be shattered repeatedly. Why was this?? Simply put it was the belief system that everyone was living by. It was one person, Roger Bannister, that changed that way of thinking. Once he broke the 4 minute mile barrier, it's now been done thousands of times, even my high school athletes.

Look at Michael Jordon what did he do and what was his belief about himself when that high school coach told him he wasn't good enough? In business what about Walt Disney? He had a dream that nobody believed. Who would ever have thought that he could build the likes of the amusement parks and business that Disney has become. What do you think the values and beliefs where of these gentlemen? So I ask you what is it that you have within you that you are capable of???

If you are a young athlete this may seem weird and strange of what I'm talking about so I would suggest you sit down with your parents, coach or even reach out to me I will be more than willing to help you through this process. This is where some of the other principles of this book and of success start.

They start right at the basics of really understanding who you are and who you need to be to become that person you desire to be. Put the work into answering the questions throughout this chapter and I sincerely believe like myself, you will find the results very rewarding when you put in the work to make the changes required. GOOD LUCK!!

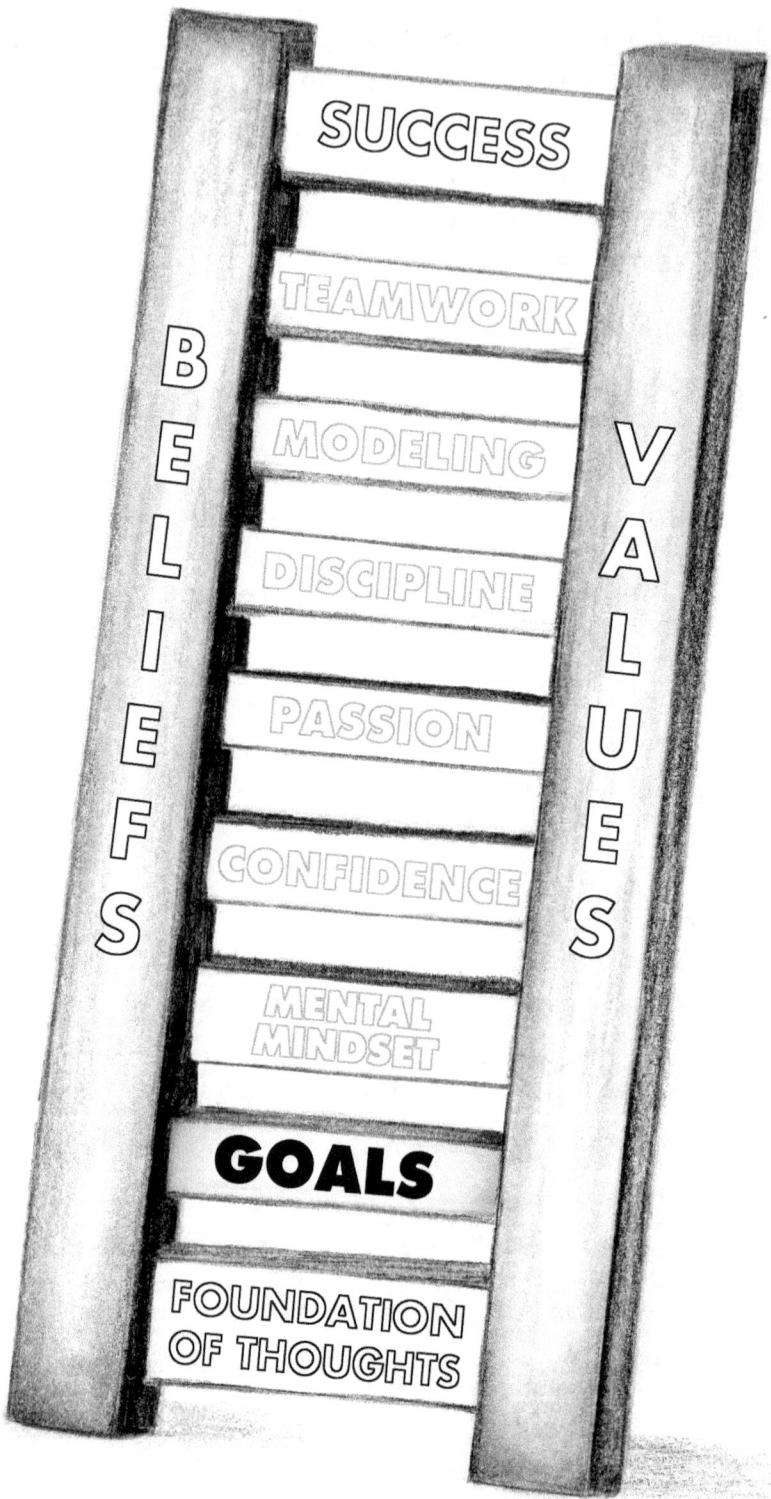

Chapter 3
GOALS & DREAMS –
The Starting Point

What is a *Goal?* What is a *Dream*? You can think of either of these as a vision of what you want in your future. It can be tied to what you want to achieve or what you want to be, do or have. Examples of dreams include being a professional athlete, being a successful business owner, having loving relationships, or having a wonderful family. Each of us has dreams. The big question is: Are they just *Dreams*, or can we make the decisions in our lives to fulfill them, to make them a reality – to bring them to life? Just as important, are you designing your life, or are you being influenced and sidetracked by outside circumstances or other people, are you conforming to society? Do you have a plan to acquire all your *Goals & Dreams* in your life? Do you have the road map or a blueprint to achieve that you so desire?

When youths are taught and learn the importance of goal setting, this valuable skill will pay great dividends in the sports they play. It will pay even greater dividends in the real world as they grow older and encounter the opportunities in the "Game of Life". Having clearly defined goals is a driving force to achievement and the first rung on the Ladder of Success.

Most professional sports teams develop game plans for each game they play. Similarly, when a pilot gets into a plane to fly you to your resort vacation, they don't just get in, start the engine, climb into the air, and let you tell them where you want to go. They know their route in advance, and they enter a flight plan into the plane's computer to get from one destination to another. It's not any different for you. Your mind is your computer and it needs to also be correctly programmed. It is my Goal with this book to help you do that. It's in your best interest to have a "*game plan*" for your life and whatever you want to accomplish. This way, you have a definite direction you're heading towards.

As Stephen Covey illustrates in his book "*7 Habits of Highly Successful People*," you must "begin with the end in mind." This means that you must know your destination. I was once at a goals seminar and the speaker asked this awakening question: "What do you want written on your tombstone?" Both of these people are really saying the following: If you want to know where you're headed, know your final destination. In five, ten, or twenty years you will certainly arrive somewhere; will you be saying to yourself, "I wish I would of or should of?" It's now time for you to design your Destiny and not just let it happen.

Our goals and dreams are the first step towards our final destination, and to get there we must know where that destination is. Think about your desired destination; is it to become a world champion in your sport, a multi-millionaire, a loving and caring parent, a devoted spouse, or a successful business owner? Is it something else? Each person has a different thought of what they want out of life, of what means the most to them. What do you want out of your life?

Success is certainly different for each of us. What is desired or considered as a success for one person could be what someone else maybe not even have an interest in, therefore, to them success is something entirely different. As you go through this book or as you go through life do not be distracted or be side-tracked by someone else's thoughts, wishes, desires or even their feeling of what success is for you. *You are your own unique person so be YOU and be all that YOU can be.*

Once you know what you want, you are stating a **Goal**. Each of us has many goals we want to achieve. If you take a close look at your life and what you want for yourself and your loved ones, you could actually determine that you have goals in several areas. These areas could be economic or financial, relationships, health, career, or personal development. Anthony Robbins simplifies it to just three areas: personal development, things goals, and financial goals. To keep it simple, his way of thinking is to ask, "What do you want to be, do, or have?" In reality that is what it really boils down to: to be, to do, and to have.

"Set your Goals high, and don't stop till you get there."
– Bo Jackson

Before you can go any further, though, you really need to know what you want. Just as a pilot can't set a flight plan into the plane's computer until he knows the destination, you can't design your life until you have a clear picture of what you want for your final destination. Your life is like a motion picture and your achievements will be remembered by many. You will leave your legacy one way or another, so why not design your life in the way you so desire? There is no point to doing as many people do – *letting it just happen*. Take control.

"The future belongs to those who believe in the beauty of their dreams"

– Eleanor Roosevelt

Try this exercise. Take a few moments to close your eyes and totally relax by taking some deep breaths. Focus first on your breathing to relax completely; then, think about the life you want to live. What images and ideas come up for you? What do you want to be? What do you want to do? What do you want to have? Hold on to these thoughts and images for a while before taking a deep breath and opening your eyes again. At this time right them down, journal them for future review. Do this simple exercise weekly to confirm you are finding your true purpose and desire of who you choose to be, do and have. More on this later.

At some point, most of us realize that we are not doing what will get us what we are really looking for in life. When that happens, it's time to do something about it and take *action* to change. One trait that will pay great dividends is your **discipline**, which we'll discuss later in detail. For now, let's look at some options to get you to where you want to go and what you want to be, to do, and to have.

The *action* is what you're looking for to create your path to achievement. This can also be described as which goals you have in place to get there and what you are doing to reach your goals. Now is a good time to address an important question: What, exactly, is a goal? ***A Goal is a definitive statement of what you want within a specific time and space.***

"I want to be rich" is not quite a goal because it doesn't specify what rich is. For you, is rich having five dollars in your pocket, a $100,000-a-year job, or owning a big house? The general statement also doesn't say when you want to be rich. You could be rich the day before you die, and that would be achieving your goal, but is this what you really want? A better way to rephrase the statement is: "I want to have a net worth of 10 million dollars by January 1, 2015." This clarifies the amount of money you want and also provides a specific time frame.

A sports example could be for a coach to say, "I want to coach a Championship Football team." This is a worthy goal, but not a well-defined one because there's no mention of when he wants to achieve this. How about stating this instead: "I will coach a group of well-rounded athletes so we can achieve a NY State Division A title by December 15, 2015." Can you see the clarity now?

Similar to a decision you make when you decide to go on vacation, you need to have a plan as to where you want go, what you want to do, and how you will get to where you are going. It's like the pilot having that flight plan or the professional sports team having a game plan. You need to have this same kind of plan if you want to achieve any **Goal** or **Dream**. It's these small Game Plan Goals that will compound to give you that 1% shift in what you are presently doing so that you will achieve the **goal** you are **disciplined** and **passionate** about achieving.

To start this process you need to know where you want to go or be, or what you want to do or have. You need to know what your destination is. Without knowing this you will have no sense of direction. If you have written your Goals down, now is a good time to take a look at them. Are they specific and complete with regards to what you want to do, how you plan to get there, and by when you will achieve them? If not, now is the time to rewrite your goals. If you don't have them written down now is the time to do so. Having them "in your head" will not be enough for you to focus clearly on them throughout your day.

Take a minute to take *action to expand, clarify, and complete the written expressions of your goals.* By writing them down, you will substantially increase your success rate than if you simply thought about them. You increase your chances for success even further by stating your goals aloud on a daily basis.

If you haven't done this exercise, you are lacking a very important **action step** required to achieve any **Dream** or **Goal**. It's vital that you do these small exercises. They are the starting point to getting in the habit of doing what you need to do to succeed in anything. It is your choice to design the life of your dreams, but it takes action, hard work and commitment to gain great rewards. Be assured that it's well worth it. Designing your own Destiny or Legacy is better than having someone else or a group of people do it for you.

Goals are the starting point of all achievement. If you have not set goals in the past, you are not alone. The number of people who do not use or set goals is large. Then there are the people who set goals to some degree but do not set them with clear, definite details, including a time frame. Or they set a goal but neglect to work on a plan or take action required to achieve the goal. When they don't achieve anything, they make excuses, saying that, "Goals don't work." In reality, *they* are the ones who *didn't work*. They didn't take action. They lacked the drive to take required action. When a person fails to reach goals, what happens to their self-esteem and self-confidence? The downward spiral begins. Don't get yourself into that situation. Be a **doer**, not a follower. Take action to get started on your dreams and goals.

Without having a clear vision of the details of your goal, and without writing it down and focusing on it daily, the likelihood of achieving this goal is very slim. I know from my own experience that this is accurate. That **was** how I used to lead my life, but I've changed. I made a commitment to set clearly defined goals and take action to attain them by using a written "Game Plan."

If you're already achieving goals, then keep doing what you're doing! But read these tips anyways as you may find some or all to be beneficial. I've successfully used the tips I present here, as have many athletes and business achievers, among others. Some pointers I developed myself and others I've heard about from successful achievers. My feelings have always been that it never hurts to follow the lead of successful people before us. In other words, "If they can do it, I can do it."

Do you think that Donald Trump, Sam Walton, President John F. Kennedy, Dale Earnhardt, Venus and Serena Williams, Mickey Mantle, Babe Ruth, Michelle Kwan, or Michael Jordan just let it happen? What about the 2010 Super Bowl Champions, the New Orleans Saints? They had a game plan. Every successful person and team develops clear written goals of what they want out of life. They design their lives and start with one goal. When they achieve that, they move on to the next, and the next, and the next, thus, creating their legacy, their destiny. They take each victory or loss and build upon it.

I'm sure that if you could look back at the lives of each successful individual, you would find that all of them had many unexpected detours along the way. It's the same as a pilot who doesn't necessarily fly in a straight line from point A to point B; they make corrections for wind that may push them off course from time to time. It's the same with life. The obstacles or challenges that come along will push each of us off course. A loss in a sporting event could be one of these obstacles, but that doesn't mean we give up and quit. No, you learn from what went wrong, get back on course after the detour, and continue on your journey.

> *"I learned that if you want to make it bad enough,*
> *no matter how bad it is, you can make it."*
>
> *– Gale Sayers*

A good metaphor is this: "The best laid plans of mice and men often go astray." This is so true when it comes to the direction we go through as we endeavor to achieve our goals. Through my analysis of successful achievers I have found that *to reach a goal you must first have a clear vision of exactly what that goal is. It first must be specific in detail as well as having a definite timetable for its achievement. And you must ALWAYS BELIEVE the goal is attainable.*

The importance of having that clearly defined written goal can't be expressed enough. I have found that once you have set a goal and start on the journey to accomplish it, that goal may change or evolve. You may reach a point where you realize you're following a goal that's significantly different from your original goal. That's okay. It could be that the original goal put you on a path that opened up a perspective of what you really want to be, do or have. I myself have gotten discouraged when I have not achieved my goals in the past, but once I learned that we need to revisit our goals and redefine them every so often, I understood goal achievement better. Not everybody achieves all their goals, but it's the people who can figure out what went wrong along the journey and make the necessary corrections that reach their final destination.

An important point in goal setting is realizing that after you have set a goal, you can't simply stand aside and say, "Well, I have this goal, so I'm on my way." You can't expect everything to just start to come together for you. Other than not having a specific goal, the biggest reason people don't reach a goal is that they fail to take the first step, which is to take ACTION.

At this point I want to caution you: Whether you are a youth or an adult, it's far too easy to become *overwhelmed and get frustrated and discouraged*, which in the long run will kill the possibility of ever achieving any goal. To avoid becoming overwhelmed and wanting to give up, be sure to chunk down the goal into small bite-size, manageable steps that will give you a sense of accomplishment while boosting your **confidence**. This in turn will give you the desire to keep reaching for the stars. More on confidence soon.

Coaches, be sure to create manageable steps in youth sports. Don't drill on hitting homeruns if the kids can't even hit the ball out of the infield. Youth players should focus on tasks that are small and manageable at first so that they gain a sense of accomplishment and then build on that. Taking small daily steps will lead to better development with greater accomplishments in the future. A great way to look at this is the 1% Rule. In essence if you have youths focus on developing one skill, move, or part of the game until they can execute it to near perfection, that one small part of the sport will compound the skills they will develop further on in their growth as they keep playing. If a player can work on improving by just 1% on a daily or weekly basis, then over the course of playing the game a few years they will show substantial improvement, thus gaining self-confidence.

> *"Do not let what you cannot do interfere with what you can do."*
>
> *– Coach John Wooden*

"You need to walk before you can run" is a metaphor that I use to get this point across to the kids I have coached in the past. Be sure you really understand and can achieve the basics before you go on. Don't have a pitcher trying to learn how to throw a screwball if he can't get a fast ball over the plate.

You can stay on track when you have clearly written, well-defined goals.

Have you created a list of what your goals are? Are your goals clear and specific? If not, revisit them again and rewrite them in greater detail and clarity. Take the required action and put this book aside right now and getting your clearly defined Goals written NOW!!!!

Don't read another word — GO DO IT NOW!!!!!

Once you have done that, it's time to focus on the steps you can take to help you better achieve them. In youth sports as well as in life you must take your goal and chunk it, breaking it down into smaller and more easily achievable goals. In essence you will have your large main goal, which may be to win a state wrestling, basketball or football title, for example. But to do that you first need to win at the local level. You can't achieve that, however, unless you first show up. By this I mean not just going to practice and working hard. Sure these are important, but you need to be all there, including mentally. You must have **Discipline** and work towards your goal on a daily basis (more on discipline in an upcoming chapter). In other words, to win you first must have many other pieces of the puzzle fit together. With these pieces in place, you are better poised to win that title.

A note to parents and mentors: For younger athletes, such as those in elementary school, your aim is to introduce the practice of goal setting by starting with smaller, simpler goals. At this age and this level of sports, you don't need to go into great depth, but introducing these concepts is beneficial. If you can get eight to ten-year-olds to start working on small steps, it can pay huge dividends for them down the road. The 1% Rule applies to all of us no matter what the age. A **Goal** of raising someone's **confidence**, for example, may sound miniscule, but it will have a compound effect as they grow older. Using a simple, age-appropriate goal is a great way to start introducing valuable goal-setting concepts: develop a goal, write it down, revise it as needed, take action towards achieving the goal. With each player, review their goals. Keep it light, and make sure they're receiving joy from being able to overcome an obstacle or achieve something they haven't in the past. No matter what, in youth sports be sure to have fun. A coach can be very helpful in working with a parent to make this happen for the player.

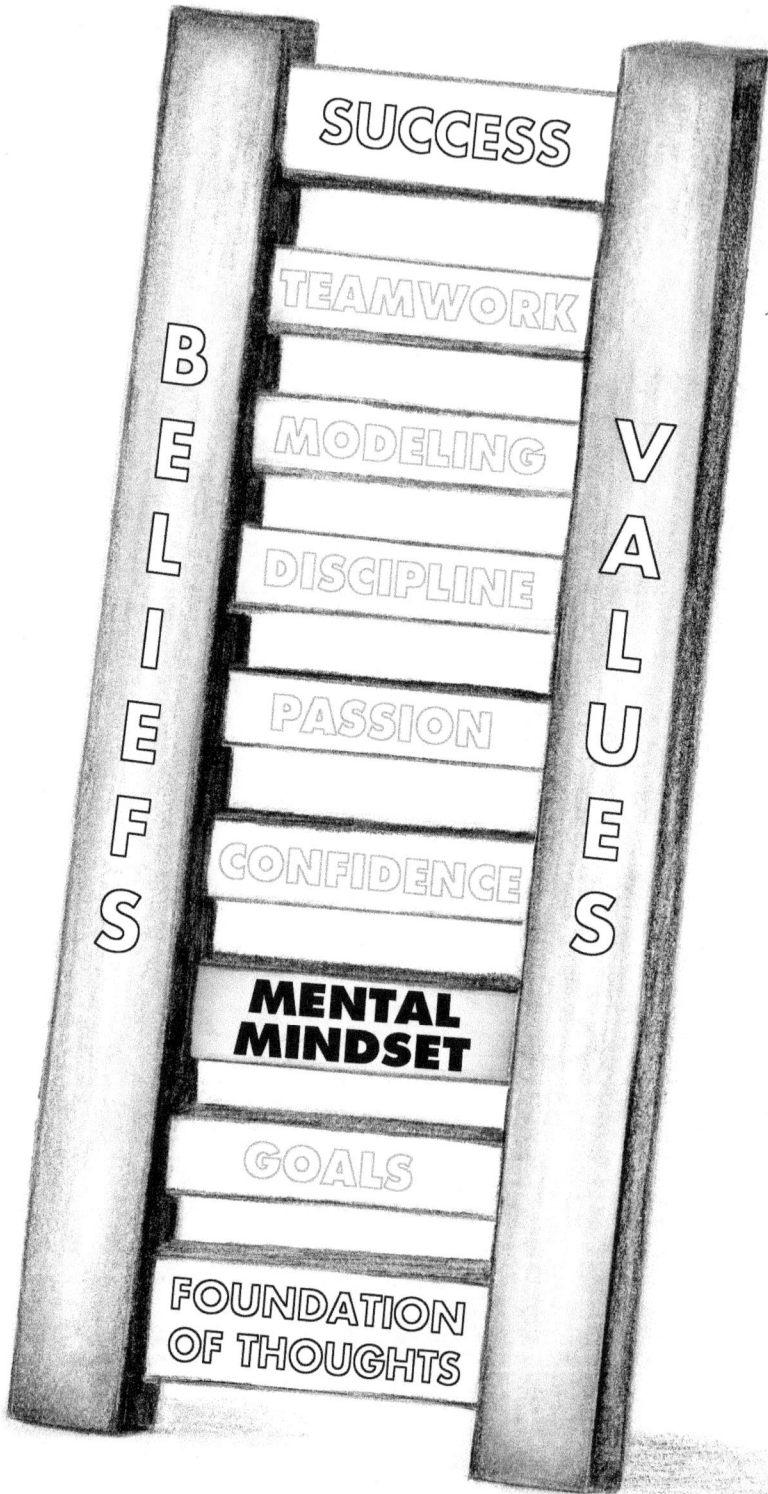

Chapter 4

MENTAL MINDSET –
The Inner Game

To build yourself up as a Champion, you must develop the *mental skills* to control your conscious thinking and not allow subconscious thoughts to stop you from reaching and receiving all that you dream. Part of developing the right *Mental Mindset* is establishing the discipline to not let outside influences or limiting beliefs stop you or knock you off your path. It's about mastering your "inner game" to give you the best results possible.

Remember my story of stepping on that wrestling mat after 33 years? I had to really work on my Mental Mindset. As I ran out to that center circle I had to face my competition, who was an extremely fit 28-year-old Marine with arms twice the size of my legs. Not only was he in better shape than me, he was also 22 years younger. That day I had to learn really fast how to develop greater Mental Toughness. Without this mental preparation, I would not have lasted even twenty seconds in that match. I believe it was because of my *mental mindset* of working hard, being *disciplined*, and building my *confidence* that I was able to make it till the end of the match. Did I win? Heck yes I won! Not in the traditional sense – I didn't win on the score board, even though 2-1 is not bad for a 50-year-old man, but I won in the "Game of Life" as I have used this experience as a learning tool to achieve more in my life.

After watching the 2010 Winter Olympics, watching some kids mentally defeat themselves in our local sectional wrestling tournament, and looking back on my 2006 wrestling experience, it really hit me how much a person's **Mental Mindset**, which I also call "***The Inner Game***", determines the outcome of a competition. The understanding of your mental mindset ties very closely with your belief system. As you will see these principles all start to tie together as they are all tools to use not just individually but also in unison to build a positive productive belief system. You must have faith in trusting that inner voice.

> ***"90% of the game is Mental, 50% is Physical."***
>
> ***– Yogi Berra***

In talking to many coaches at many levels of sports, as well as reading about some of the most successful coaches and players in professional sports, it has become very clear to me that a large percentage of any game, match, or competition is "mental." This should be a large part of coaching in every sport, at any level. The mental mindset of any and all players affects the outcome of the event, therefore, more time should be focused on this during the preparation phase, whether it's at practice or just before stepping foot into competition.

The mind is a crucial part of sports success or failure. I have seen many youths get taken out of a sport due to the fact they are not mentally prepared for what they are about to face. I don't particularly agree with this approach. Instead of pulling a kid out of sports, parents and coaches need to prepare themselves for a loss while teaching every player that it's not so much about winning – it's about doing one's personal best.

As I have stated many times, especially with youth sports, you need to take a loss or a win as a learning experience and grow from it.

Learning how to create and use visualizations and affirmations is a vital aspect of developing greater mental toughness. When you visualize yourself accomplishing a Goal, your mind does not distinguish between whether or not it's real. Once your mind envisions this accomplishment it will come up with ways to achieve it. This shows the power of your subconscious mind. Practicing visualizations of success will greatly bolster your likelihood of attaining any accomplishment. The use of visualizations allow you to see your success in advance thus making it easier to achieve.

When you add positive, deeply felt affirmations or declarations to your success visualizations, you will feel so much better about yourself, believing that you are able to achieve more in life. When you repeat these affirmations you are actually playing a legitimate trick on your mind, as your mind cannot tell the difference between imaginary success and real success. When I first heard of this a few years back I had probably the same doubts you might be having. However, having read and heard this concept in many books and seminars, I decided that all these successful people can't be wrong. I gave it a try and over time I did start to feel and see the beneficial effect these practices have. Will you see and feel changes overnight? No, but give it time. Be patient. It took years to program your mind to what it is today and it will take time to reprogram it. Be committed to these small daily changes and, like me, you will find the results can be overwhelming – in a very good way!

For youth to understand the importance of these simple exercises is vital to overcome the setbacks that most adults have had due to the programming of the past limiting beliefs that we had inputted into our subconscious mind. I urge parents and coaches to bypass the programming of our past and encourage our youth to use visualizations, affirmations and declarations to build their mental mindset of belief in themselves.

When you read or hear about successful people in any venture you will find that they have one trait in common: All are *laser focused*. This takes a tremendous amount of mental preparation. They are mentally tuned in to their Goal and all the steps they need to take to achieve that Goal. They have great mental clarity regarding what they need to do. They have a team of players to help them along the journey. And very importantly, they have a *"don't give up"* attitude. You see, it all starts in the head. It's what lies between your two ears that will determine what you do with your life. This is a very important aspect of achieving anything you wish. If you let outside influences affect your daily practice of what needs to be done, you are letting someone else control your thinking and your thoughts. Be strong and powerful with what you allow to enter your mind and control you. Your mind is the most powerful thing you have within yourself, so be cautious of how you use it.

Here is an example of youth understanding the power of mental mindset. As I explained our son, Kyle started racing go-carts/microds at age 8 and moving up through multiple size cars till he started racing Legends at the age of 12 with adults at close to 100 mph, he found out the hard way of what happens when you lose or don't focus. His first realization of needing to be focused came when we were practicing one night and a friend who raced professionally came to practice to help him learn the sport.

We first talked about how you had to locate points on the track, specifically in the corners that you had to hit so you can drive efficiently through the corner without scrubbing off speed. My friend would then go out and actually stand at a spot in the middle of the corner and told Kyle to run right up tight to him to hit this spot on the track. *Now you talk about being crazy this guy really had faith in Kyle to stand there and risk his life.* Well, in short this made Kyle really learn that to maintain maximum speed he had to be focused every single lap. This is the same as a batter learning to focus on the baseball coming out of a pitchers hand, the football receiver being focused on running the exact same pass pattern as the quarterback had called for or even the soccer player that was passing with clear focus of where his team mate was running to so they could receive the pass. Focus is needed in all sports at every level.

This then led to him realizing that it took time for him to be able to be prepared to do this doing a whole race. So the next thing we realize over the course of the next few weeks he was always wanting to go to the entry to the track before each race really early before his race. After this going on a few times I started to realize you couldn't talk to him or even get his attention, he was getting mentally prepared, or some say "Getting in the Zone". This is when he would visualize what marks he had to hit on the track. To see it in advance helped him to be better prepared when he had to react in split seconds to what may be happening during the race. What started out with a simple explanation now had turned into a new ritual or practice he had acquired.

Fast forward a couple years in a newer division and another faster car that he is racing in a national race along the east coast. There was this race in Concord NC that he was in where he ended up with the fastest time and had the pole position, which means starting first when the race begins for you non-race fans. So, naturally before the race he wants to be sure he is on the grid early. There was no way you could distract him, he was on a mission. Well the race starts, coming around turn 3 into 4 he gets hit in the right rear and gets spun out and fly's across a manhole in the infield. Now you can just imagine how this 11 year old felt, he was upset and over the two-way radio I could tell he was crying. So as a parent so many things rush through your head: make sure he isn't hurt physically, is the car damaged in some way and is it save to continue.

Well, after the judges decide Kyle was placed at the back – dead last. A penalty for which he did nothing wrong, I guess we have all felt that's happened to us all at some time. By now we realize the car tends to be fine so it's now time to re-set, to get down to business, so it's now time to stop the crying, respect the judge's decision and fine a way to make the best of it. It's at that time Kyle found he didn't have a lengthly period to get in the zone now it's go time.

Without getting into all the details Kyle found a way to be so focused and determined that by lap three he was back up front. He then went on to win that race. But that wasn't the real lesson he learned. The real power showed up 2 weeks later at another race in North Carolina. Upon arrival at the track the night before Kyle was able to walk the track with the race promoter to discuss the track banking. At this time he heard about the adults who came earlier in the day and how 2 of them crashed due to the combined banking in turn 3&4. Well, the next morning we go out to practice, keep in mind Kyle is always first on the track. So after a few warm up laps they get the green flag to reach full speed, then as Kyle enters turn 3 I see his path is to high so I hold my breath. Just as I expected right into the turn 4 concrete outside wall then back across the track into the inside concrete wall. Off the motor home I go. As I arrive at the car the safety personnel are finally getting him awake from being knocked out. Other than a wrecked race car, a broken ego and a concussion Kyle learned a very valuable lesson. You see he thought that just because he had just won this big national race a few weeks earlier he felt that this race was in the bag, so to speak. He learned that his past results didn't dictate his future results and lastly that even though he was at the top it didn't mean he could stop focusing, being in control of his mental mindset. He found that just a split second could mean life or death in a race car. It's through his years racing that we feel he is so focused and committed to succeed in all aspects of his life now. Kyle learning to focus through sports and these racing experiences we believe has helped him in his adult years.

This is true for all sports. The power of your mental mindset can be taught through any sport. As I illustrated one simple exercise of having Kyle hit his marks during practice turned into a very valuable life skill that at 24 has already paid dividends for him.

*"It's in moments of decision that you
shape your Destiny."*

– Anthony Robbins

Developing the right Mental Mindset to give you an advantage with your Inner Game involves a multi-point approach. Whatever your goal may be, keeping your mind fine-tuned and laser-focused involves staying physically and emotionally healthy, too. To be at the top of your inner game and your chosen sports, try the following:

A.   Have a clear and precise fitness workout plan that relates to your sport, both an aerobic and anaerobic fitness program. An internet search can yield many ideas for creating a program that will work for you and your particular sport, or you may wish to consult a personal trainer.

B.   All professional and Olympic athletes will tell you to make sure that your diet provides you with the vital nutrients needed to perform at your peak performance. Create and adhere to a healthy diet that best relates to your sport. A nutritionist can be extremely helpful with this.

C.   Maintain a weekly schedule that will focus on the basic fundamentals of your sport. You need to develop the fundamentals before proceeding to the next steps of development. The basics should flow naturally.

D.   Set up a time to meet in person or over the phone with a Mentor/Role Model or Accountability Partner on a weekly schedule. This will keep you accountable as you strive to reach each small Goal to make sure you are on track with your Big Goal / Dream. It is not uncommon to find yourself off track from time to time. In the earlier example of a flight plan, pilots find themselves having to adjust due to changes in winds and airflow currents. You will find that you will also have to adjust to changes along your journey. It is ultimately how you face this adversity that will determine how far you go in succeeding all that you aspire to do, in sports and in every phase of your life.

E. Keep track of your training program. I have found that most individual, local, and state champions go above and beyond. They have their own drills, exercises, or fitness program that they do in addition to their regular team practices. It's this kind of discipline to go above and beyond that builds professionals in any sport. It's the character of a Champion to do more than what the competition does. Develop your training program and keep a record of your actions on a daily basis so that you have a reference as to what is working and what isn't. When something isn't working, immediately make the changes that are necessary.

Remember, though, that preparing your Mental Mindset is not just for game day. It's not just for sports, either; it's for every aspect of your life. Keeping your Mental Mindset strong and healthy involves daily preparations, including:

1. Having clearly written Goals that you read and visualize daily with passion.

2. Reading aloud with emotion twice daily your affirmations to increase your level of self-confidence.

3. Develop a daily practice of specific focus to your task at hand. This is not only true in sports but in all aspects of life. When this is done as consistent daily practice it then becomes a habit and will create lasting long term results.

Again, be sure to take these daily actions to stay Mentally focused and clear on the end result, whatever your Goals or Dreams may be.

A Note to Parents And Mentors: To help our youth fully understand this principle of Mental Mindset, there needs to be a mutual understanding between parents and coaches that it isn't all about the win. All parties need to serve as Role Models and the support structure to give players the tips, the tools, and the understanding of learning from whatever the outcome may be. With younger children, how parents and coaches handle youth sports can determine whether or not they continue in sports as they grow into their high school years. As kids get older, fewer participate in sports. In some cases this is perfectly fine; these youths have reached an age where they've determined their interests lie elsewhere. However, it is a fact that there's a percentage of dropouts leaving sports due to negative experiences they had at a younger age. It could be that they were ridiculed for making mistakes, or they haven't been shown what they need to do to correct what they've been doing wrong. Maybe they never got the encouragement to try again. Most adults give up on trying to accomplish a specific task or goal if it doesn't come easy, so why would we expect our children to be any different? Youth, just like adults, need to stay focused on their Goals and Dreams to be able to achieve them. To see youths mentally beat themselves up in competition is totally disheartening. That's why staying on top of the "Inner Game" is vitally important.

This leads to a point I want to stress about helping youth achieve their goals even to a small degree. Youth need help and guidance to see right from wrong in a loving, compassionate environment. They will learn nothing if they are yelled at, made fun of, or belittled. My wife, who has worked with children her whole life, has the most compassion and patience I have ever seen. The older I get, the more I see what she can get children to accomplish, and it is totally amazing to me. A young student or athlete can reach a level above their initial skill level if you take the time and patience to work with them. Isn't this what youth coaches are really there for? A coach's role is similar to that of a parent when it comes to teaching and guiding. Coaches are to serve as role models and lead by example. It will take hard work by each player, the whole team, the coach, and the parents for everyone to develop a healthy *Mental Mindset*, but it is well worth the extra effort.

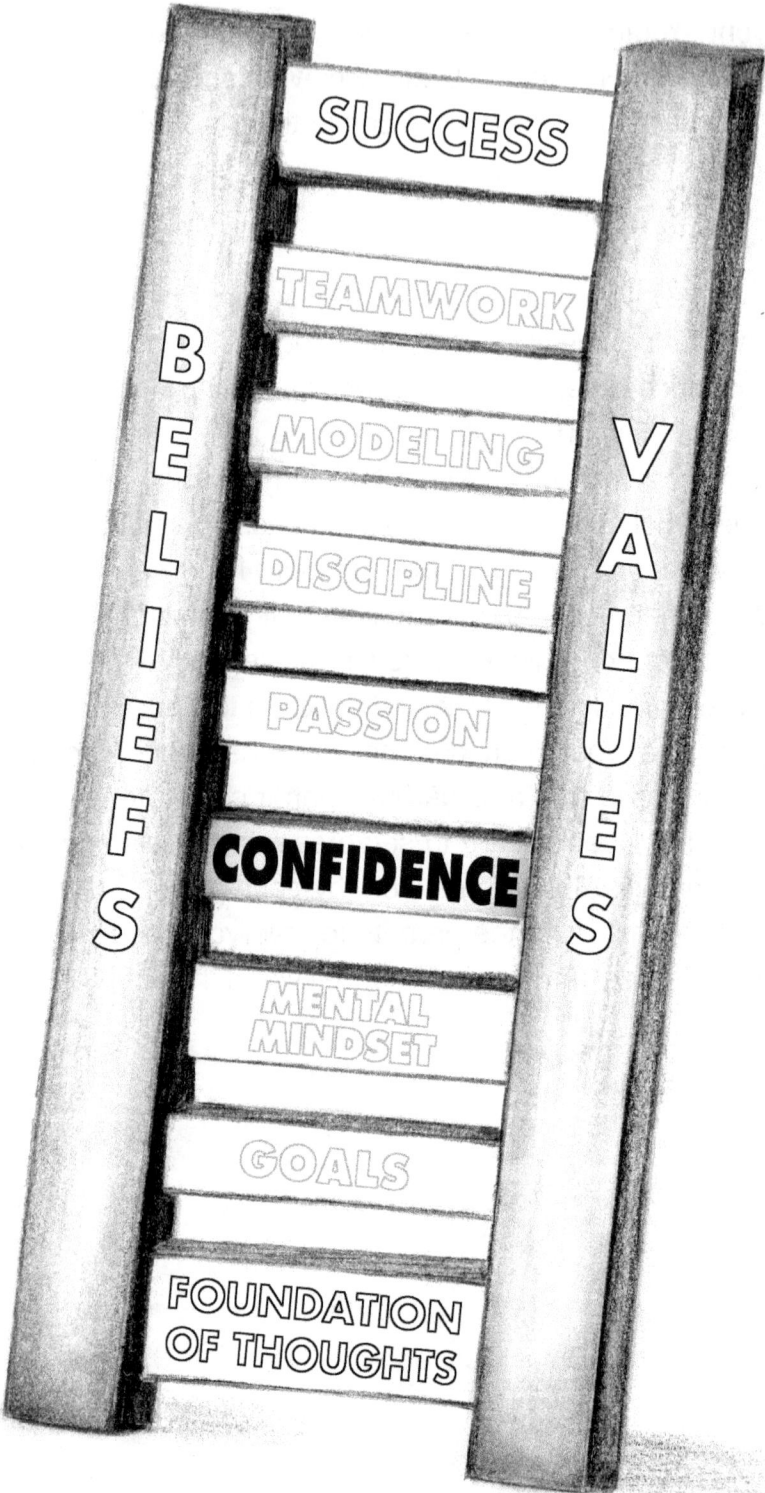

SUCCESS

TEAMWORK

MODELING

DISCIPLINE

PASSION

CONFIDENCE

MENTAL MINDSET

GOALS

FOUNDATION OF THOUGHTS

BELIEFS

VALUES

Chapter 5

CONFIDENCE –
The Backbone to Achievements

Youth players in any sport are the same as adults: We all need confidence to achieve what we wish to acquire in our lives. Confidence is the **inner strength** that will guide you along the journey.

Confidence is one of the more important principles that determines whether young athletes achieve their potential in sports.

When kids lack confidence, they doubt themselves, play tentatively, are very reserved in their play, and are hard on themselves. The result is that most kids often lose their motivation to improve. Ultimately, these barriers keep them from enjoying sports and they end up giving up playing sports and thus start a downward spiral of not having a belief in themselves.

If you are a parent or coach you play a critical role in determining whether your youth athletes feel confident. What you say, what you do with your hands and body during games or competitions will affect your kids' confidence.

Here are some of the top confidence killers for young athletes:

- They hold unrealistically high expectations of themselves. They put demands on themselves in regards to how they are to perform. Eg. "I need to score 20 points in today's basketball game."

- They call themselves negative names. Eg. I'm not strong enough to play football."

- They tell themselves "I Can't" statements. Eg. "I can't score when I play against this team."

- They doubt their abilities, they are unable to overcome their limiting beliefs in themselves. Eg. "Can I really make that shot?"

- They worry about what everyone thinks of them. Eg. "Coach is going to bench me if I don't play well. My girl-friend is here watching and may not like me if I don't play well."

Most all youth athletes struggle with at least some of the above confidence killers.

However youth can learn how to overcome these confidence hurdles and perform with confidence. They need to build up their self-confidence. This is not just vital in sports but in all that they will need to face in the "Game of Life.

If you don't have **self-confidence** you basically are in an area of disbelief; you incorrectly feel that you don't have what it takes to achieve what you are going after. If you don't have belief in yourself, you're in essence giving in to failure before you ever start.

This disbelief can be called *limiting beliefs as I mentioned earlier*. Such limiting beliefs can manifest in many different ways. In youths they may appear as, "I'm not as good as my opponent," "He or she is bigger than I am," or "They're better than we are," just to point out a few. These thoughts are a diminishing factor to any achievement. You must be able to overcome these limiting beliefs to be able to build **confidence** so that you can achieve your **Goal**. Again one's belief system is what ultimately shapes your reality. Have faith and walk boldly in your beliefs. This is where there needs to be a firm understanding that the principles of mental mindset ties with your values and beliefs to give you the **confidence** to move forward with courage, faith and enthusiasm that you are not only capable but also worthy of achieve that which you so desire.

Once you are aware of what these *limiting beliefs* are, it's time to work on overcoming them. This is why Values and Beliefs have such a vital part in supporting your Ladder of Success. These limiting beliefs will weaken the support rails needed to reach the pinnacle of any Success. A primary way to do this is to create a visualization and affirmation that you repeat to instill the belief that you need to achieve your Goal. We've talked a little bit about affirmations previously. But what exactly is a declaration or affirmation? Simply put, it is a statement of belief that you repeat on a consistent basis to erase the limiting belief in your conscious and subconscious mind.

Creating your own list of affirmations and declarations can be a starting point to change the mind's programming that we all developed as we were growing up. These thoughts were programmed into our minds by what we were told or experienced, some of it sound but some of it completely off the mark. Through frequent, consistent affirmations, we can break free from limiting beliefs over time. We can reprogram our minds and keep what's working, delete what's holding us back, and add what will propel us higher.

Parents and coaches, the manner in which we interact with each other, as well as how we talk to our young athletes, will have an impact on them not just in sports competitions but also in almost every aspect of their lives in the future. There is a correlation between respect and confidence. Won't a higher level of self-confidence be more beneficial for youth in every aspect of their education? It will give them a better feeling about themselves when they're taking a test or completing homework assignments. It will set them up for success at a young age so that this will be the norm for them as they grow through the teen years into adulthood.

Does a lack of self-confidence impair someone when they go in for a job interview? You bet it does. Companies are interested in people who have a high level of self-esteem and can follow directions and complete tasks without hand holding. Managers don't want to have to babysit employees or stand by to inspire them to get their work done. Getting the job done is important in team sports, too. The lineman who blocks for a quarterback on the football field is there to protect the quarterback, and it's vital that he does his job well. Each player has to have full confidence in the other. Everyone on the team relies on each other, so each individual must have enough self-confidence, discipline, and skills to do his job right. The coach, the quarterback, and other players need to have faith that the linemen will do their job. The whole team relies on the coach doing a good job. The linemen protect the quarterback and, in turn, expect the quarterback to do his job and help score points for the team. Everyone depends on everybody else doing their job confidently and expertly. Everyone needs to feel a sense of pride in doing his job to the best of his ability while having the confidence that he can do it. Self-confidence in youth sports, like self-confidence in the business world, in academics, or anywhere else, leads to greater personal and team success in the "Game of Life."

"Besides pride, loyalty, discipline, heart, and mind, confidence is the key to all locks."

– Joe Paterno

Let's take a closer look at the subconscious mind. Recent brainwave testing shows that your subconscious controls 96% to 98% of your daily activities. Understanding *why* we do *what* we do can help us develop new habits to reprogram old conditioning. Confidence is one of the keys to successful reprogramming. Coaches, first analyze what level of self-confidence your players have and what limiting beliefs they may need help in overcoming. Then, help your players focus on conscious decisions and actions that will benefit them individually and the team as a whole. Developing confidence can propel anyone to achieve their Goals. Being confident helps in achieving success in all we do and as you hopefully see there is a direct relationship with ones level of confidence and their level of **Mental Mindset** control. A person's *Mental Mindset* can create a "make or break" result, as discussed in the previous chapter.

Who's talking in your Head? Whether or not we're aware of it, we all do something called *self-talk*. It is basically the process that we subconsciously or consciously do to determine how we are to achieve a particular task. Do you realize that you are always talking to yourself? It is mostly your subconscious giving direction to your body to perform a specific task. Take combing your hair or taking a shower, for example. Do you consciously think about what you are doing? Do you count how many times you brush each part of your teeth? Do you think about what you have to do when you climb into the shower? Most people do not; they brush their teeth and wash themselves the same way every time without consciously thinking about specific steps. They have developed a habit that is governed by the subconscious. Through brainwave testing this has been proven numerous times. Again, our subconscious controls a large portion of what we do and how we do things.

Do we consciously self-talk? Yes, we do. Is this self-talk always done in a positive fashion, or do we sometimes ask ourselves questions that are disempowering? Envision this: you are a first-time youth player at your first practice and the coach gives instructions to perform a specific drill. You have never done this before, so as you wait your turn you stand there and start telling yourself, "I can't do that." You are not alone. This is something that even adults do at times.

If you are a parent, have you ever been in a position on the job where you had a new task to do and you didn't know how to do it, but your boss put this on your plate to do and it was up to you to complete the task? Chances are you used self-talk in this particular situation. It is the nature of your self-talk that determines how you'll get through the situation or task at hand.

"My thoughts before a big race are usually pretty simple. I tell myself: Get out of the blocks, run your

race, stay relaxed. If you run your race, you'll win...
Channel your energy. Focus."

– Carl Lewis

As Carl Lewis states above he uses positive self-talk to get himself Mentally positioned to run any race.

Now that you understand self-talk, do you see that, when done repeatedly in a negative context, it can severely affect someone's confidence in themselves? If we can self-talk ourselves into a lower level of self-confidence, surely we can turn things around and use it to elevate ourselves to higher levels. This is where affirmations and declarations come into play.

As I mentioned earlier, youth players – like anyone – will and do have many limiting beliefs. Just the other day in a wrestling match, one of our young wrestlers told me, "I can't get that takedown." My response was, "Can't is not in my vocabulary, so I don't understand what that means. However, 'I will go do my best' is what I like to hear!" Actually, I'm glad he verbalized his limiting belief because it gave us the opportunity to make a correction. He was able to replace his 'I can't' with 'I'll do my best,' a much better perspective. I gave him an affirmation to repeat to himself whenever he felt scared or worried going into a match: "I am going to go for the takedown to the best of my ability." Does this mean he will get it? No, but he will start to build a greater inner belief in himself that in time will pay great dividends. In conjunction with the affirmation we then did a visualization exercise to let him actually visualize a takedown in the process and for him to see himself succeeding. Repeating this visualization over and over again helps his sub-conscious mind see it as reality, therefore, giving his conscious mind the tools needed to complete the successful takedown with confidence. The visualization process let's you see your success in advance – a powerful tool.

I pointed out to this young wrestler that if he focuses on mentally saying this affirmation to himself while practicing takedowns, he will build his self-confidence and see his success rate start to increase. As self-confidence grows, a higher level of accomplishment normally results, which in turn creates a positive emotion. Whether it's happiness or joy, the new emotion will help override negative feelings within oneself. We need to find every way possible to create positive emotions in all youth athletes to help them build their self-esteem and self-confidence.

> *"You need to play with supreme confidence, or else you'll lose again, and then losing becomes a habit."*
>
> *– Joe Paterno*

Negative self-talk comments create the limiting beliefs that youths end up putting into their subconscious. The negative feelings then develop into bad habits. These bad habits during practice then end up showing up during competition. To keep matters from escalating, work on noticing bad habits during practice and actively correcting them. Likewise with self-confidence; once you have determined what's driving you (or your athlete) to lack confidence, you can take steps to correct this, just as in the example with the young wrestler. Replace negative thinking with positive affirmations to create good habits in the long run.

Now let's look at the correction process. The purpose of a correction process is to create affirmations that will raise a person's level of confidence. Affirmations should be written in the "I am," "I can," or "I will" context. Here are examples:

"I am wrestling to the best of my ability."

"I am working hard at practice to better my skills."

"I can work hard in practice to build better skills so that I can go out and be a sectional champion."

"I will have total belief in myself at all times."

"I can accomplish all that I set my mind to do if I do it with 100% commitment."

Affirmations need to be positive with *no grey area*. I know some people think this is a crazy idea. Well, I can say I said the same thing not long ago. However, I have found that used consistently over time, firm affirmations spoken with conviction truly do help. As with anything, it doesn't work overnight. It's like developing good skills in any aspect of a sport; it takes practice and dedication to see results. Affirmations are best said first thing in the morning to create a positive emotional feeling in oneself right from the start, and then restated before going to bed. Studies show that the feelings and thoughts you have just prior to going to sleep are what your subconscious picks up on. Saying affirmations just before going to bed also puts you in a positive state of mind. I'm sure some readers will attest to the fact that they wake up in the middle of the night thinking of all the problems they are facing in life. Try saying affirmations and see if you sleep better through the night. Affirmations work with time as they help reprogram your subconscious mind.

When you reprogram your mind and create positive emotions about yourself within yourself, you will slowly see an increase in self-confidence. With this higher level of confidence your belief and faith about what you can accomplish will compound, thus paying great rewards. To really add to one's success in overcoming limiting beliefs, building self esteem, or even to ease into a greater sense of being able to accomplish your desired task add a visualization of seeing that which you so desire as being already accomplished or completed. When you visualize try to bring in the picture the sights and sounds and even the emotions of how you would feel by achieving in your visualization. The more senses that you can bring into the visualization the powerful it will be. Let the visualization guide you to your reality of that which you desire.

"It's lack of faith that makes people afraid of meeting challenges, and I believe in myself."

– Muhammad Ali

Faith is the belief to see the Invisible, to believe the Incredible, and to achieve the Impossible.

Coaches, sit down with each youth player and discuss with them what feelings they have about the sport they are playing and, just as important, about any other aspect of their life. Take pen to paper here and write down what limiting beliefs each youth may have about themselves. Parents, this can be a great exercise to do as a family so that your youth does not feel they are being singled out or that there is something wrong with them. Have this be a time when everyone is working on becoming a better person in every aspect of their lives, not just in sports. It can be a great family bonding exercise.

As a parent you very well know or can analyze for yourself what limiting beliefs your child/children may have. A coach can also know and/or analyze his players limiting beliefs. Once you have assembled this list of limiting beliefs, it's time to write an affirmation that can be used to turn each item into a positive belief. Make these affirmations inspiring. If your youth is very young, write a simple but powerful affirmation that you can repeat daily with them while creating a bond at the same time.

Now that you have some clear affirmations, make a commitment to say them twice daily, in the morning and then just prior to going to bed at night. Repeat each affirmation at least three times. If you have only a few affirmations, you may want to repeat them 5-10 times. I know this sounds wacky, but give it a try for thirty days. Repeat your affirmations twice daily every day for the full thirty days, and you'll see a change start to develop. Once you have completed this process for thirty days you will have developed a **daily habit**. A NASA experiment years ago verified that when a specific task is completed daily in the exact same fashion for 30 to 45 days in a row, without missing a day, a habit is being formed. However if you miss a day, the process starts all over again at day one.

Remember also to do a visualization along with the affirmations will bring much greater success.

I find myself repeating my affirmations as I'm driving or waiting on hold for someone to answer the phone. There are days when I may say some of my affirmations 15-20 times and, believe me, it has had an impact on how I think about myself. If for some reason I don't say them when I get up, I've noticed that they'll come to me when my mind is idle, giving me the opportunity at that point to go through my entire list.

If you would like to increase the effect of your affirmations dramatically, add intense emotions and feelings to them. Doing this reaches a higher level of your sub-consciousness and triggers an increased response from within. For youth this may be hard, but as an adult give this a try for thirty days, non-stop twice every day, and see if you feel better about yourself.

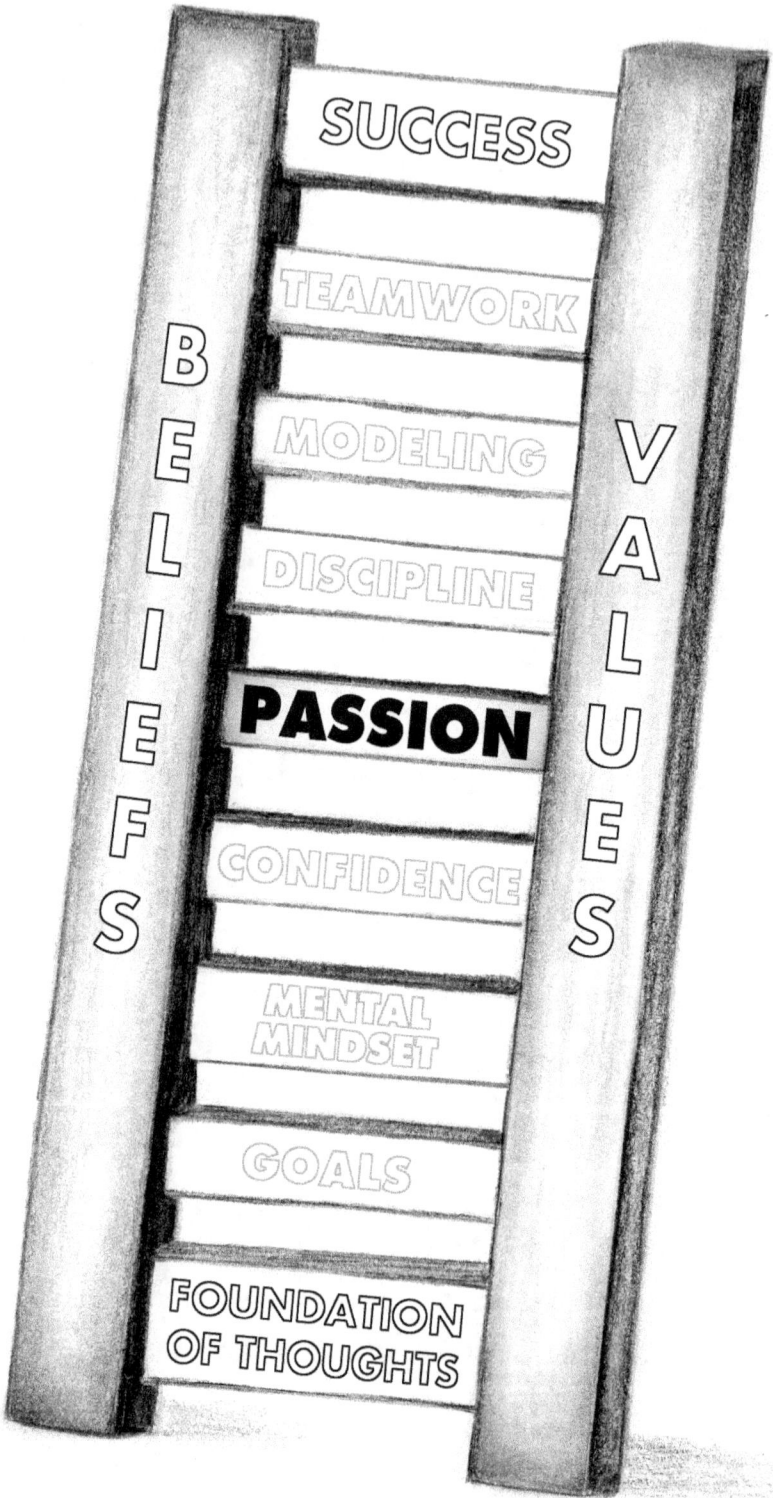

Chapter 6

PASSION –
The Driving Force

Passion is the deep feeling within that is needed to succeed. Your beliefs will build your *Passion*. You can say you have the desire to achieve, but in reality it will be your *burning desire* or *Passion* that will be the catalyst to give you the energy to reach your pinnacle of success. Let it be said that those who make reaching a dream their *Passion* are the ones who will be a step above of their competition.

Passion has to come from within. It's got to be a decision from your heart to reach deep within yourself to achieve. When you make a decision to do something or create a Goal, have you committed all you have to achieve it? Do you have the **Passion** to separate yourself from the competition?

> *There is no greatness without a passion to be great, whether it's the aspiration of an athlete or an artist, a scientist, a parent, or a businessperson."*
>
> *– Anthony Robbins*

The principles of **confidence** and **passion** work hand in hand, and you need to consciously develop both. Don't let them be controlled by any negative experiences that have ended up in your subconscious mind and influence your daily habits. Unproductive daily habits are *not* a sign of passion to succeed. The good news, though, is that your passion will help you override some of those unproductive habits.

Positive emotions and actions make up the essence of true passion. The greater the positive emotions that you process in regard to a specific activity, the greater your passion will be. Passion is the love of doing what you're doing. When you love doing something it is said you are truly passionate about it. When you are doing what you really love to do, your passion will grow naturally.

Some of the positive traits and emotions you'd associate with a passionate person could be:

Love

Excitement

Optimism

Enthusiasm

Focused

High Energy

Confidence

Purpose

Negative emotions of a non-passionate person would be:

Bored

Overwhelmed

Distracted

Disinterested

Prone to Procrastinate

Pessimist

Here is what Anthony Robbins' book "Awaken the Giant Within" says about Excitement and Passion as some of the 10 Emotions of Power:

"Excitement and passion can add juice to anything. Passion can turn any challenge into a tremendous opportunity. Passion is the unbridled power to move our lives forward at a faster tempo than ever before. How do we "get" passion? The same way we "get" love, warmth, appreciation, gratefulness, and curiosity – we decide to feel it."

Tony Robbins is the most passionate person I have known or met. He certainly walks the talk. When it comes to passion, he is the ultimate teacher to listen to.

What you focus on controls your whole life. Your focus determines your destiny. To better control your focus you need to be asking yourself the right questions, the ones that will drive you towards the direction to achieving your dreams and goals. Some questions that can help you are:

What is it that you truly want?

What is it that you love to do?

Who do you want to be?

These types of questions will direct your focus, putting you onto the path of your destiny. You will then find what your true passion is.

For youths in sports, passion is something that will develop with time. I don't recall seeing, nor do I believe, that passion for a sport will be created during the youth's first few practices or games. However, I have seen passion grow within the season of a particular sport. That's what influences the decision of whether or not to come back and compete the following year. A youth may find that they like a sport in either a first or second practice but true Passion develops over time. The main principle that will help grow passion is one's level of self-confidence. Passion will grow as the youth develops a higher level of confidence playing the game. I higher level of self-confidence will breed a higher level of passion. In my own case I believe that Passion played a huge part of pushing me to work-out and become physically prepared for that wrestling match at the age of 50. My **Passion** helped provide me with the **Confidence** to keep pressing forward.

A lack of passion for a sport is the reason that many youths drop out of any particular sport. The amount of passion that one has for doing anything is a gage or measuring device. A low level of passion will bring a low level of results, but a higher level of passion will likely bring a higher level of success. If a youth doesn't feel passion for his or her sport, don't push. Allow them to find out what they love to do – art, theater, reading, science, math, or any area of their choice – and help them develop a passion for this. By helping them determine what they love to do, you're helping them determine the direction that they are heading as they venture out into the real world. To live fully to the highest level in the "Game of Life," passion is needed, one of the powerful 7 Success Principles. **Passion** is the driving force of achievement.

In many surveys taken of youth athletes they say usually the number 1 or 2 reason they play youth sports is to just "have fun". This truly exhibits that no matter what we are doing "enjoy the process"!! As adults I belief we start to lose sight of how important this is. As I coach I even fell into the trap and lost sight of the simple reason most all of my elementary youth wrestlers where wrestling was because they wanted to do something with their friends and to have fun doing it.

This came to light when one year when we had so many kids crying after matches, parents yelling at their kids in frustration and us coaches not having any fun or enjoyment in the process either. It's not till one week I decided to try something. We made a shift in our practice's, we took the last 20 minutes of practice for 2 weeks and made games out of drills or just played some crazy made up game to let the kids have fun. We then took that laid back approach to the weekend tournaments. We would go and do our best but in the end we wanted to the kids to enjoy the moment – to have fun along the journey. The results blew us coaches as well as the parents away. In the very first tournament we had kids win matches for the very first time. In the second tournament we had kids not only win matches but ended up in 1st or 2nd place. It was amazing the way this little shift brought so much success to the kids, the parents and enjoyment to us coaches also.

I believe we had helped the kids fine the passion in the sport. They found that is has met their need of having fun in a passionate way. In addition, we helped the parents realize the kids need to do what they love to do and when they do the rewards are far greater. When parents push their child into a sport that they don't enjoy or are passionate about how can anyone expect them to be successful.

If you are a parent or a coach please take the time to ask the questions of your child or athlete if they are really in love with what the sport offers them. At the elementary age they are looking to have fun. As they hit the middle school age that shifts depending on each individual child and yet at the high school age it may still be to spend time with their friends, however, for others it may be that they have the vision of making it a career or at least playing at the collegeant level. Ask the questions of your young athlete so you can help them find success and enjoyment in the game vs being frustrated and beat-up by failures and setbacks.

Now as most adults know, but sometimes we forget, ones passion or love for doing something can change. Let me say for myself years ago I loved building, I better have as I did it for over 40 years, however, presently the passion I once had for doing it for a living has diminished. I still love using my hands but it's not there in the same strength as it was years ago. Now my passion is helping youth understand who they really are, guide them in finding life lessons through sports and my life experiences, and help them find their passion so they can be the best that they can be!!!

So if you ever come to a point that yourself or a child seems to want to change direction in sports or life rest assured that this is normal. More than anything, as my Mentor Tony Robbins says, "LIVE WITH PASSION"

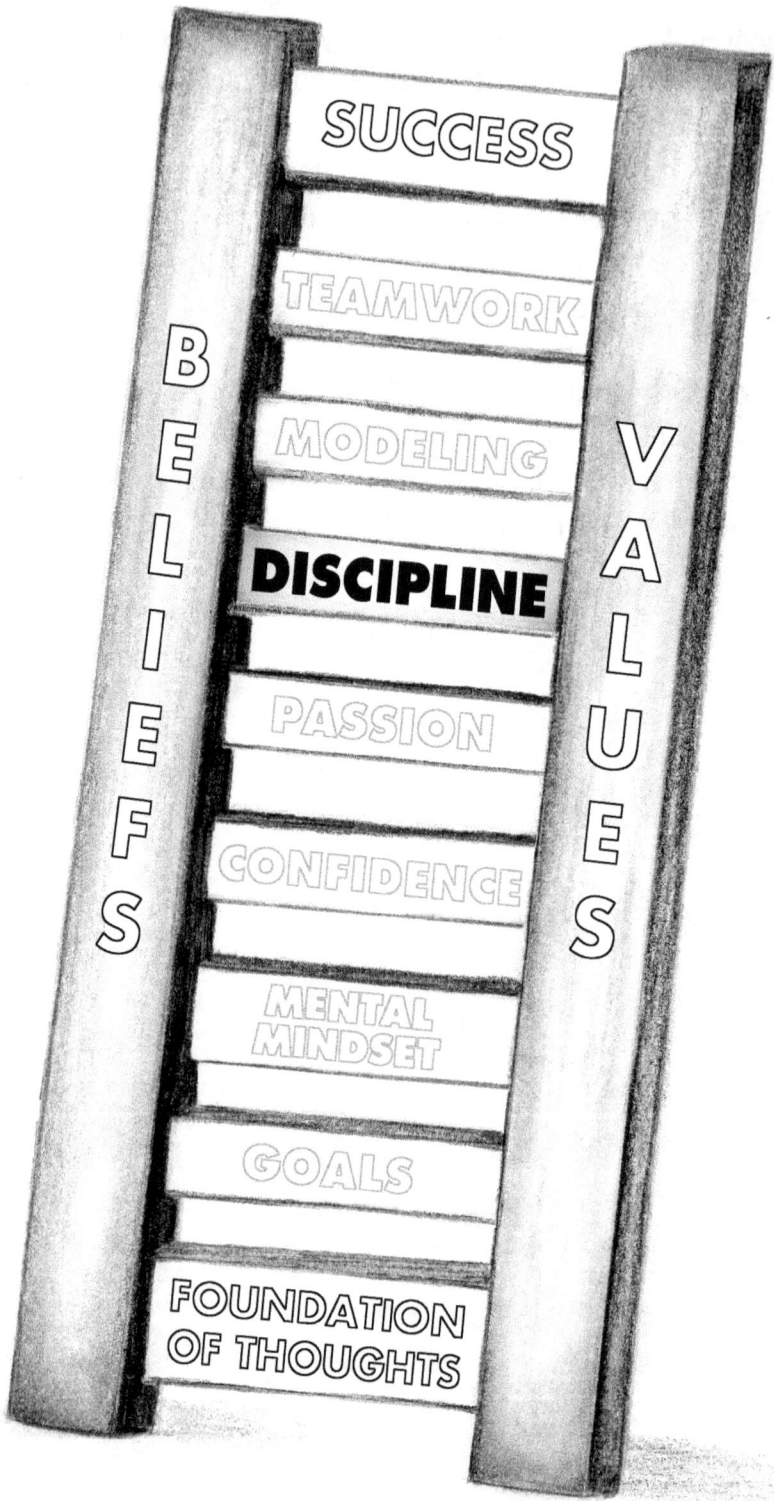

Chapter 7
DISCIPLINE –
The Guiding Light

Discipline is the steering wheel that directs you along the course you are heading. For most youth they look at Discipline as being yelled at or being told what to do. This is not the Discipline that is referred to when you need to be disciplined to achieve a Goal. It may be better understood by youth if we talk about it as being **Self-Disciplined**. With the use of **Self-Discipline** you will have a better sense of direction, therefore, have a better chance of achieving all that you desire. If you are like most of us, and certainly like every participant in youth sports, you need to be disciplined to stay on track and not be influenced by outside pressures. We all know that it is easy to sit down to watch TV, to go play video games, or to hang out with friends. Spending too much time on these activities, though, will keep you from reaching your dreams. It is **Self-Discipline** that will keep leisure activities such as these in check. We all need free time, time to relax and have fun, and *by all means* youths need plenty of it. But we also need to make the time to work towards our goals. **Self- Discipline** is the tool that youth need to keep them from going astray, to stay on track, and to not be led down the wrong path with peer pressure. **Self-Discipline** is what you need to keep excuses at bay, to not let an excuse for not doing or accomplishing something of any size large or small. Someone with self-discipline will be able to overcome the desire to let excuses impede their success.

Just as self-discipline is the key to success, the *lack* of self-discipline is the major cause of failure, frustration, under-achievement, and unhappiness in life. It causes us to make excuses and sell ourselves short.

"Self-discipline is the ability to do what you should do, when you should do it, whether you feel like it or not."

– Elbert Hubbard

Self-Discipline is the strength from within that will determine what you do on a daily or even hourly basis. It is these decisions that you make on a consistent basis that you need to control. Discipline is needed to guide anyone down the correct path. Practicing the principle of discipline is needed in every aspect of achievement. Whether it is youth sports or the "Game of Life," discipline plays a huge part in success.

Developing success starts with disciplined steps of achievement. Discipline is about maintaining healthy behavior, and with regards to achieving dreams and goals it is the guidance to stay on task to reach the ultimate goal. Staying committed to achieve your goals is a disciplined action.

Self-discipline has also been called, *self-control*. Your ability to control yourself and your actions, to control what you say and do, and to maintain behaviors that are consistent with your long-term goals is a sign of a well disciplined person.

Youth players are like adults; if we don't have a disciplined approach to overcoming the obstacles before us, we will never achieve the highest success possible. Discipline is the power to push forward and demand more from yourself. To go after all that you think at first is not possible. You can achieve almost any Goal you set for yourself if you have the discipline to pay the price, to do what you need to do, and to never give up.

"There are only two options regarding commitment.
You're either IN or you're OUT.
There is NO such thing as life in-between."

– NBA Basketball coach Pat Riley

Discipline is misunderstood by adults and youth alike. To most youth, discipline means getting "yelled" at for doing something they shouldn't be doing. We need to be taught that there is more to it, namely self-discipline. Achievers of all ages need to learn to have self-control to stay on track and to refuse to be led down the wrong path. Some of the wrong paths that youths fall into are drugs, drinking, crime and isolation. The paths that many youth take can also be due to peer pressure.

Youth sports can be a great tool to keep youth away from bad influences. Drugs and drinking don't mix with success in any sport as they will severely impact one's physical abilities. Most teams have policies against drinking and the use of drugs. At the professional level the use of drugs and drinking can be controlled by random testing, however, at the youth sports level the best means of control are parents, coaches, and education. Youths need to be educated about the pitfalls of the use of drugs and drinking.

With involvement with drugs, drinking and even crime the short term gain will severely impact the greater reward and that is long term gain. It's not uncommon for most people, youth and yes, even adults to look at the short term reward or fun time vs the end result of hard work creating long term rewards. This is where true discipline plays a vital part of one's success.

The wrong path of crime, drugs or drinking can come from peer pressure or, as the saying goes, "being mixed up with the wrong crowd." When youths are involved in sports they have less time to go out and get into trouble. Any youth who has been involved with the wrong crowd can be influenced by a sport to change their ways and walk along the right path.

Isolation is not as common, but the youths who isolate themselves have been found to have very low self-esteem, a lack of self-confidence. This is one reason they isolate themselves. If you can get them to try a sport even to a small degree, you may find that they have hidden abilities. Or they see that other youths have some of the same issues that they have. Once again the principle of confidence comes into to play. Low self-esteem is not like an incurable disease. By changing one's beliefs in themselves, their self-esteem can be raised. This can be done through helping them explore a hidden talent or skill within themselves. You must always have a profound believe in yourself to be successful in *anything* that you do, whether its sports, a hobby, a career path or even everyday activities.

The path of self-discipline for any person is critical to the accomplishments in their lives. The path to achieving your dreams and goals is governed by your ability to stay focused on the steps you must take to succeed in all that you do.

"I'll always be Number 1 to myself."

– Moses Malone

The easiest way to look at having self-discipline is basically developing the right *habits.* It's been said that "successful people have the habits that unsuccessful don't have." So how disciplined are you to have and/or create the habits to go above and beyond what the competition is doing? The Discipline to stay on track and stay committed to successful habits will have positive long term results.

Take the time now to review your daily habits and rituals and see what habits that you need to change or develop that will steer you in the direction that you need to go to achieve that ultimate Goal. Create the self-discipline to not let outside influences distract you from achieving all that you desire.

Napolean Hill wrote "**Self-discipline is the master key to riches**." Self-discipline is the key to self-esteem, self-respect, and personal pride. The development of self-discipline is your guarantee that you will eventually overcome all your obstacles and create a wonderful life for yourself.

It's been said that some people are just born with natural talent. Whether it be sports, dance, singing or some other talent if you don't use it and keep up with the changes that the body goes though you lose the advantage of what some people say is being "born with God given talent". If that is the case can't the same be said for developing talent? How is the best way to develop a talent in any area of life? That is disciplined daily practice. A disciplined well practiced dedicated individual can have greater success then someone that has lost their discipline to remain at the top of their game.

It's paying that price for success that will pay great rewards. As stated earlier, it does take a great deal of discipline to stay focused on what that Goal or Dream is. It doesn't matter if its youth sports, college sports, professional sports or a career, to be the best of the best it will mean dedication to do more than others are doing to be at the top of your game.

The use of discipline will develop higher levels of self-esteem, self-respect, and personal pride. As you move yourself up the ladder of success you will find that your developed **self-discipline** has changed your character into a stronger and greater person. When you can make the **Disciplined** changes necessary to reach for the stars and achieve your dreams you will find that you have become a person that you thought that you would never be. You have overcome what you thought was impossible and it's for that reason no matter what the accomplishment you are a *Champion*! Again, **Discipline** is one of the most vital principles of achieving Success.

So what disciplined action plan do you life by? If you don't have discipline steps that keep you on task to achieve your Goals it's now time to develop a plan to keep you disciplined so that you can achieve all that you desire. Be prepared to pay the price as the rewards will give you an amazing feeling.

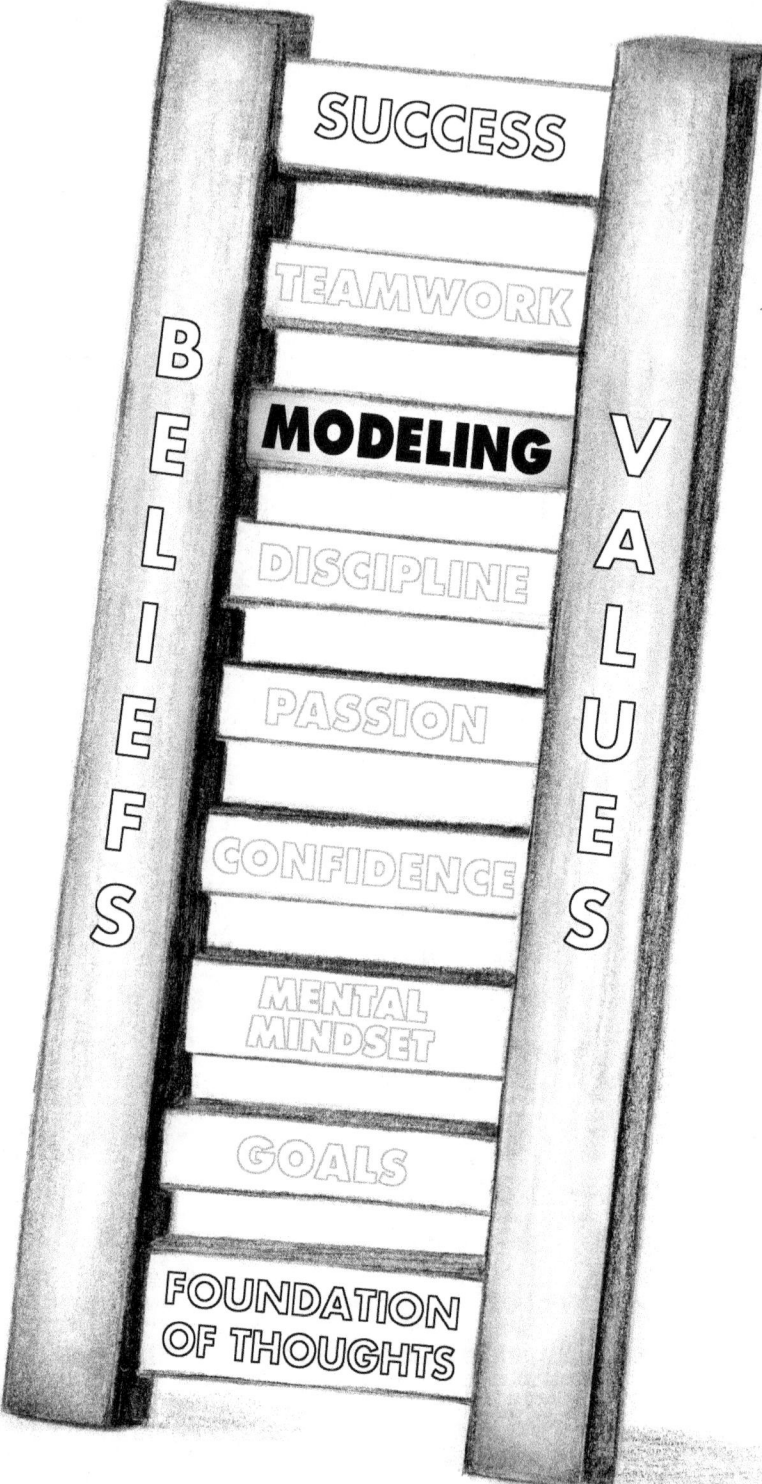

Chapter 8
MODELING –
Follow the Leader

Why is it that the Olympics have been going on for hundreds of years and every four years there are new records set? Why is it that at one point no one thought that anyone would break the four-minute mile and yet, once it was broken, thereafter it was broken numerous more times? Analyzing what those record setters accomplished gives those who follow the guidelines to succeed in the future. In fact, these achievers can light the path to success in whatever you choose to achieve at any level in sports as well as the "Game of Life." They **Model** success for the rest of us.

What is a **Model**? A **Model** is a representation of something. So a **Model,** or better yet a **Role Model,** is someone who represents a particular trait or achievement that you could follow or copy. A **Role Model** is someone who has achieved something that you want to also achieve. A Mentor is one who can guide you down the path of who or what you want to Model. Ideally, your Mentor is also a Model for you. This is the best possible scenario as the Mentor has accomplished what you want to also accomplish, and therefore, they can provide direct insight into how they did it.

A Mentor who is not a Model gives information that is secondhand; it may be good information, but it is not optimum. Nevertheless, any Mentor can provide great insight whether or not they're a role model, so don't rule out the use of a Mentor as they are still better than doing it alone. Your Mentors and Role Models are part of your Success Team.

Parents and coaches need to be role models. In addition, youth will reach out to find the right role model or mentor in their sport at a skill level above their own. This could be a high school player, a semi-pro player, or even a pro. As a parent or coach, you can help your youth look for someone who has a good work ethic and the values that you think youth should be following. We are all aware that even at the pro level there are some so-called professionals who would not lend themselves to being a good role model for our youth. So guide your youth well when they seek role models. Having a positive role model will give them a path to follow and the understanding that if someone else has accomplished it, they can too.

"You have to expect things of yourself
before you can do them."
– Michael Jordan

An excellent example of a good role model is Michael Jordan. If you look into his life you will be amazed that he didn't start playing school ball till later in high school, but with his work ethic and determination, look at what he has achieved. There are people like this in almost any sport, so if you do your research you can find someone to use as a good model for reaching dreams. This holds for adults as well as your children.

Helping youth choose someone to Model is like providing them the paint to create the picture of their Destiny. Earlier we talked about visualizations; the Role Model that they choose will allow them to visualize a clearer picture of what they may be working to achieve. Like an adult wanting a new Porsche; you could look in a magazine to get that picture or, better yet, go to a dealer and get your picture taken sitting in that car of your dreams. Having that clear picture enables anyone to visualize with much more clarity.

You need to realize that your subconscious mind *cannot* distinguish between a visualization and the real thing, so the more you practice visually seeing something in your mind's eye the easier it is for your mind to work on helping you achieve it in reality. This is just one of the many aspects of understanding how your mind really works. The more you learn and understand the basic principles of how the mind works, the easier it is to understand why and how affirmations, declarations, incantations, and visualizations work like they do. The role of any Mentor or Role Model is to provide guidance so the receiver can learn by example the process that one can take to achievement. Role Models have created the path and have shown the way so that all you need to do is follow it.

Your role model's past success can give you a clear visual picture of the achievement. Visualize what you can of his or her achievement, of what you are trying to achieve or obtain. Then, replace that person in your visualization with yourself. Climb into that person, see what they see, feel what they feel as they accomplish this Goal. See yourself in your mind's eyes as having already accomplished your goal. When I reflect on the 2008 Olympics, I think of watching a few of the athletes closing their eyes and moving their bodies as if they were performing what they had to do. They were in the game before it even began, preparing their Mental Mindset. They were actually visualizing the event before it ever happened.

"Before you can win a game, you have to not lose it."
– Pittsburgh Steelers Coach Chuck Knoll

This is why having a Mentor or Role Model provides a huge success advantage towards achieving your ultimate Goal or Dream. As we spoke earlier, youths can model either a coach, an older youth that they look up to, or even a professional athlete. They can also model a parent or family friend. The objective of the Mentor or Role Model is to give guidance and insight on the direction required to proceed to a goal. They are there to help build **Confidence** and to be the guide to **Disciplined** actions that are needed as well as the crutch or secondary support system to **Goal** achievement. As you can see, the Mentor or Role Model helps the player develop critical **success principles**.

If the athlete doesn't have a Mentor or Role Model, the next best guide is what's known as an Accountability Partner. An Accountability Partner is an associate or teammate who will keep you on track to follow your Game Plan to achieve your Dreams and Goals. They are there to keep you on task and keep you focused. Two or more players can work together as Accountability Partners for the good of all by keeping each other disciplined to work towards specific Goals. All teammates can be accountability partners for one another as they can inspire each other, with everyone sharing a common Goal.

A parent or teacher can also be a great Accountability Partner. It needs to be clear, though, when a parent is being a parent vs. an Accountability Partner. The youth needs to understand the difference as much as the parent needs to provide encouragement of the principles and discipline action steps required to achieve the desired Goal.

Like a Mentor or Role Model, your Accountability Partner is part of your Success Team.

If you want a professional athlete to be your Mentor or Role Model, you may find that you will not get personal input from them, but you can still use them as a Role Model by simply reading all you can about them, "mirror" what they do if they are still active in their sport, or study them in any fashion you can. One idea is to ask them if you could watch them practice to analyze their drills and work ethic. Then go and "mirror" what they do. Watch their emotions, drive, determination, work ethic and mannerisms. All these elements are part of their "success game plan." With advances in technology, there are many ways to learn more about any professional.

Your coach can serve as a good mentor or role model. If you are interested in this option, the best thing to do is just ask. Most likely, your coach will appreciate you showing greater interest to learn more, and he or she will be willing to help.

Most importantly as a player, you must be coachable! You need to be attentive to what you are being told and take advice from your coaches, mentors and role models to work hard on what they are teaching you. Don't let distractions get in your way, because if you do, you won't achieve your dreams and goals. Hard work *will* pay great rewards with time. You need to have full belief and trust in any coach, mentor or role model. Just as you must have Confidence in your teammates you need to have Confidence in anyone that you Model. Yes it will be hard to stretch and reach outside of your comfort zone, but that is the price you must pay if you want to become a true **Champion**. Whether it be sports or the "Game of Life" you will need to trust many people and you will need to be trusted yourself.

"I have missed more than 9000 shots in my career. I have lost almost 300 games. On 26 occasions I have been entrusted to take the game winning shot . . . and missed. And I have failed over and over and over again in my life. And that is why . . . I succeed."

– Michael Jordan

A Note To Parents: As you help a youth athlete find a Role Model or Mentor, ask yourself important questions. Does this individual have a track record of accomplishing what your youth aims to accomplish? Do they have values you want for your child? Can and will they commit to working with you? The only way to find out if they'll work with your youth is to contact them. The first thing to do when contacting them is introduce yourself and ask if they have a few minutes to speak to you. If they do, then explain your reason for contacting them. Let them know what you admire or appreciate about them – what you value in what they do. This will give them some insight into the help you are looking for.

Be prepared to meet some resistance; after all, you are asking for something without offering anything in return. One thing your youth can do is ask to follow or "mirror" (also called "shadow") their role model on a particular day, especially if they are in the sport the youth is trying to learn. An elementary school youth, for example, may be able to mirror a high school student. Or a high school student can shadow a college student.

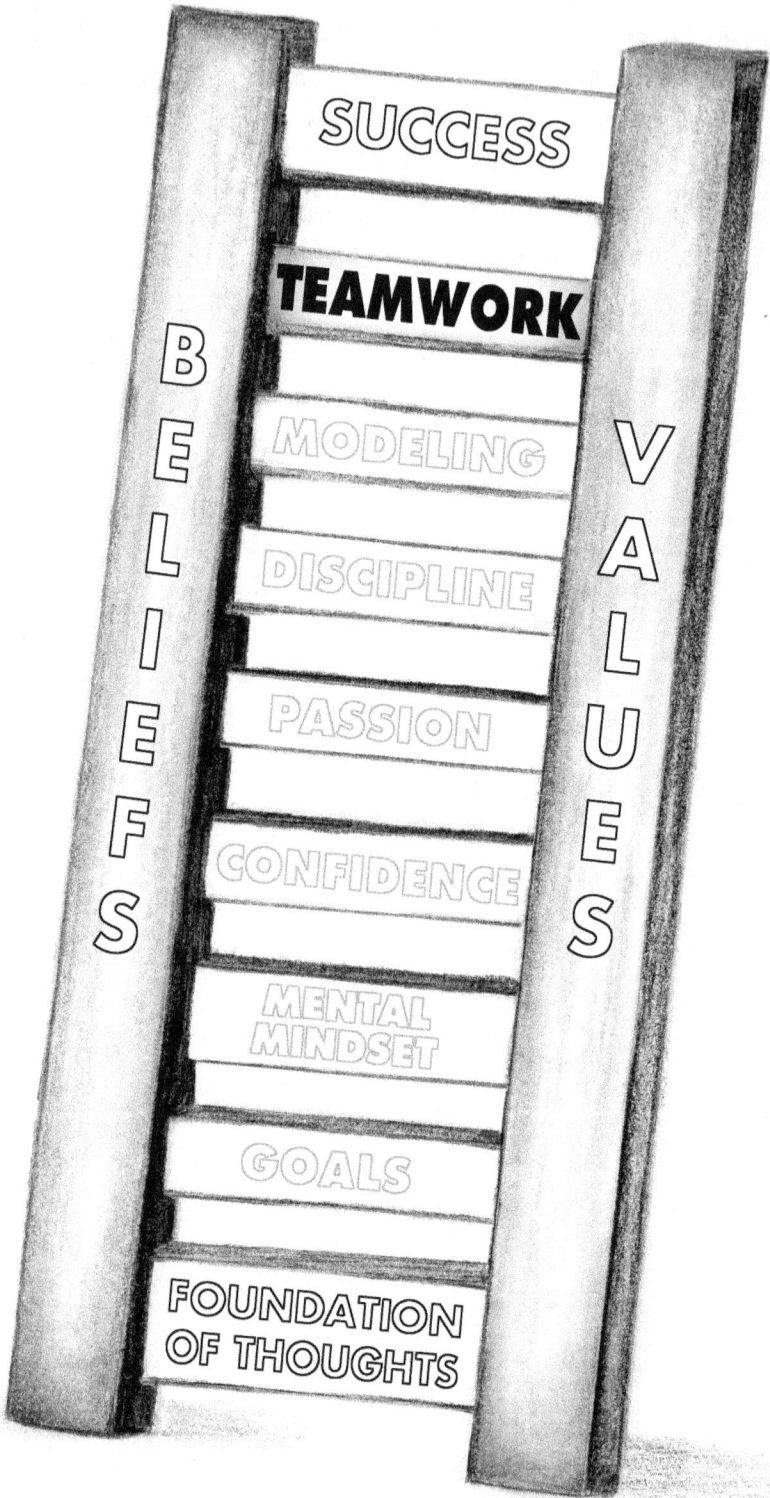

Chapter 9
TEAMWORK –
The Master Mind Effect

So what is *Teamwork*? Is it just the understanding of the players on a field of play working together, or is it the development of a team of people working together to achieve a common goal? It is everybody working together with a common goal. Not just the players on the field but also every player on the sidelines plus every coach and every parent who supports the players. It takes a group effort to achieve the common goal. From practice to the game each player needs to be part of the team. Yes, there may be the starters, but without the rest of the team where would the starters be? Don't they all go to practice and provide the support for the team? Even though a player isn't in the game, they should feel and should be made to realize that they are part of the team as much as anyone who participated. That's true *Teamwork.*

> *"Ask not what your teammates can do for you.*
> *Ask what you can do for your teammates."*
>
> *– Magic Johnson*

Whether in sports or in business, **teamwork** is a vital part of success. In "Think and Grow Rich," Napoleon Hill talks about Andrew Carnegie's use of a Master Mind. In essence a Master Mind is a Team of people working together for a common goal. Master Minds are widely used by successful business groups. I was first introduced to this concept in my reading of "Think and Grow Rich," and with further reading about successful people throughout time I have found that many, if not all, make use of Master Minds or Teams.

The development of Team Players is of utmost importance in many sports. In football, baseball, lacrosse, soccer, and many other sports you have multiple players on the field at one time who must work in unison to obtain a common goal. That's the definition of being a team player.

However, as with a Master Mind there are many other people involved in the success of a Team, including the parents and the non-starters. Looking at it on a bigger scale, as with a professional football team, we add to the team many different trainers, corporate officers, and secretaries that you never see or hear about during the playing of a game. They really are part of the Team.

In a Master Mind or business, it may be the lawyer or accountant who does the books for the company. They play vital roles when it comes to the success of the business, so they really are part of the Team. Receptionists, security guards, human resource personnel, marketers, analysts – all contribute to the success of the company. This is why I believe it is so important to teach our youth what the true meaning of Team is. It is *everybody* working for the common goal. My belief is that a Coach needs to be sure that each and every player on the Team realizes this. It doesn't depend alone on one's own skill level or what part they play on the Team; *everyone* is a part of the Team at any level of participation. I believe this important point is getting lost in some programs, and it will be detrimental to the program in the long run.

In order for every player to develop, they need to have game time. It's been documented that many youth players drop out of sports due to a lack of playing time. It kills their self-confidence, a vital principle of success. When they lose their self-confidence they don't see a need to continue to participate, and their future development is severely impacted. Even though a player may not be a starter, he or she is still part of the team and must be included. To give these players even the smallest portion of game time could end up showing them what is within them. No one really knows what someone is capable of doing without being given the opportunity. Keep in mind that you only need to win by one point at any level, so why not give the whole team game time experience? It could pay huge dividends down the road.

I had an opportunity to coach at a professional football players youth camp about a year ago. It's was certainly a very rewarding opportunity to be part of a team of coaches from the elite high school teams whom had won many state titles, to college coaches of all levels and even retired NFL players there volunteering their time. Then again, her I am never coached a day of football in my life. I believe it was due to the first edition of this book and my past years of coaching multiple sports that got me the opportunity.

During this 2 day camp I had 12 young men 11 and 12 year olds to work with on my team. During the first few hours the 26-28 teams of kids would rotate from coach to coach doing drills. Thank God for them that I was given a playbook to follow, lol. Then we would get our own team back for 30 minutes of practice before we played 3 games of touch football. It was during that time I knew I had to coach them on what I knew best and that was it always boils down to basics – the mental aspect of the game – so I took 2 minutes and told them when my son was their age he raced race cars and if he wasn't focused and confident that he could he could crash and possibly kill himself. Well, you can guess that gave them something to relate the importance of focus to being that my son was their age. On top it, it really peaked their interest in how did he do that. We discussed what the vision of the team needed to be. A quick 3 minute visualization exercise for them to see and feel victory just as my son needed to see that checkered flag at the end of every race.

I then explained it was about teamwork, he and I doing our individual jobs for the benefit of getting the best result on the track. So it all boiled down to each of them playing totally focused on the job for the benefit of the team. In addition we only played 10 at a time so it meant that 2 boys where always sitting out. Therefore, we made a rotation for that to happen. During the first game we worked on staying focused and as a team player being sure you sat out with no complaining when it was your turn. I ended with this, "there was to be NO negativity it was about being a team player and being respectful for your teammates and be focused on your position as you did the best you could do, that was all any of your teammates and I could expect from you."

We tossed the ball around for a few minutes, got together with a team cheer and on to battle. Not for one minute did we work on any plays or any other strategy, that came on each play called by the quarterback on offense or the deep defender on defense. Kept it clean, basic, and simple!!!

I have to say by the time the second game was at half time the kids were yelling "stay focused" and working together subbing in and out as needed, I never had to say a word after that game. In fact, at times I had more kids out then we needed to have a few times.

In the end by the time we finished playing 6 games over 2 days we ended up undefeated and in the Super Bowl. As you could expect a few ex-NFL players wondered how I could end up in the Super Bowl as I had never coached football. As I say many times it's the simplest parts of any sport that make the greatest difference and it all starts right between our own two ears. It starts with just following simple principles. Of course it helps when you have young men that had the desire to listen and learn, they did one heck of job those 2 days. BTW we even played the second day without the best skilled player who was our quarterback the first day. The kids handled the transition very well as they had built up confidence the day prior as well as they played as a team very well.

Teamwork is not just what takes place during the game. It's everything that starts from the origination of the goal. Giving every participant a vital position on the team will give each player a sense of accomplishment. When one wins, the team wins.

Have you ever watched a professional football team and heard the announcers talk about the 12th man? They are referencing the fans. The fans' noise will help disrupt the opponents. The disruption that the 12th man can create on the opposing team has more than once affected the outcome of a game. From this example, do you see how the Team spans a broad spectrum? Each member plays a vital role in the accomplishment of any goal. Now let me clarify this. This may be the case in professional sports but it's my belief that in the youth sports arena the 12th man should NOT be the distraction but instead the motivator for both teams. Remember, it's *youth sports,* they are not professionals with million dollar contracts. They are youth looking to have fun but at the same time can learn those vital skills and principles that will be ever so important to them as they develop and grow,

Be sure to clearly define these roles to help you better understand not only your job but also the job of everyone on your team. Support them as they support you.

Each team member must learn to be compassionate towards everyone else on the team. Everyone will have a bad day once in a while and it's the teammates' responsibility to lift that person's spirits and help them get through the problem at hand. If you just miss a goal and your team loses, you'll feel bad and you'll appreciate moral support. Therefore, you should be a leader and offer that same support to others.

"Ask not what your teammates can do for you.
Ask what you can do for your teammates."
– Magic Johnson

You may have noticed that I use the above Magic Johnson quote more than once. I repeat it due to the importance I feel it has in youth sports. It is an essential aspect of creating winning teams.

So who is on your Team? It's now a good time to sit down and make a list of your complete Team. Does your Team include any or all of the below:

- Your Team Coach

- Your Parents

- A Mentor, Role Model or accountability Partner

- A fitness Coach

- A nutritionist coach

- A position specific coach, if applicable

Be sure that all your Team members are aware of the outcome you desire. What is your **GOAL**? Once you are all on the same page and derive a "*Game Plan*" you then will need to push forward and overcome any obstacles that come up along the journey. It's your "Team" that you can rely on to help you do this. Good LUCK!! SEE YOU ON THE PODIUM!!!

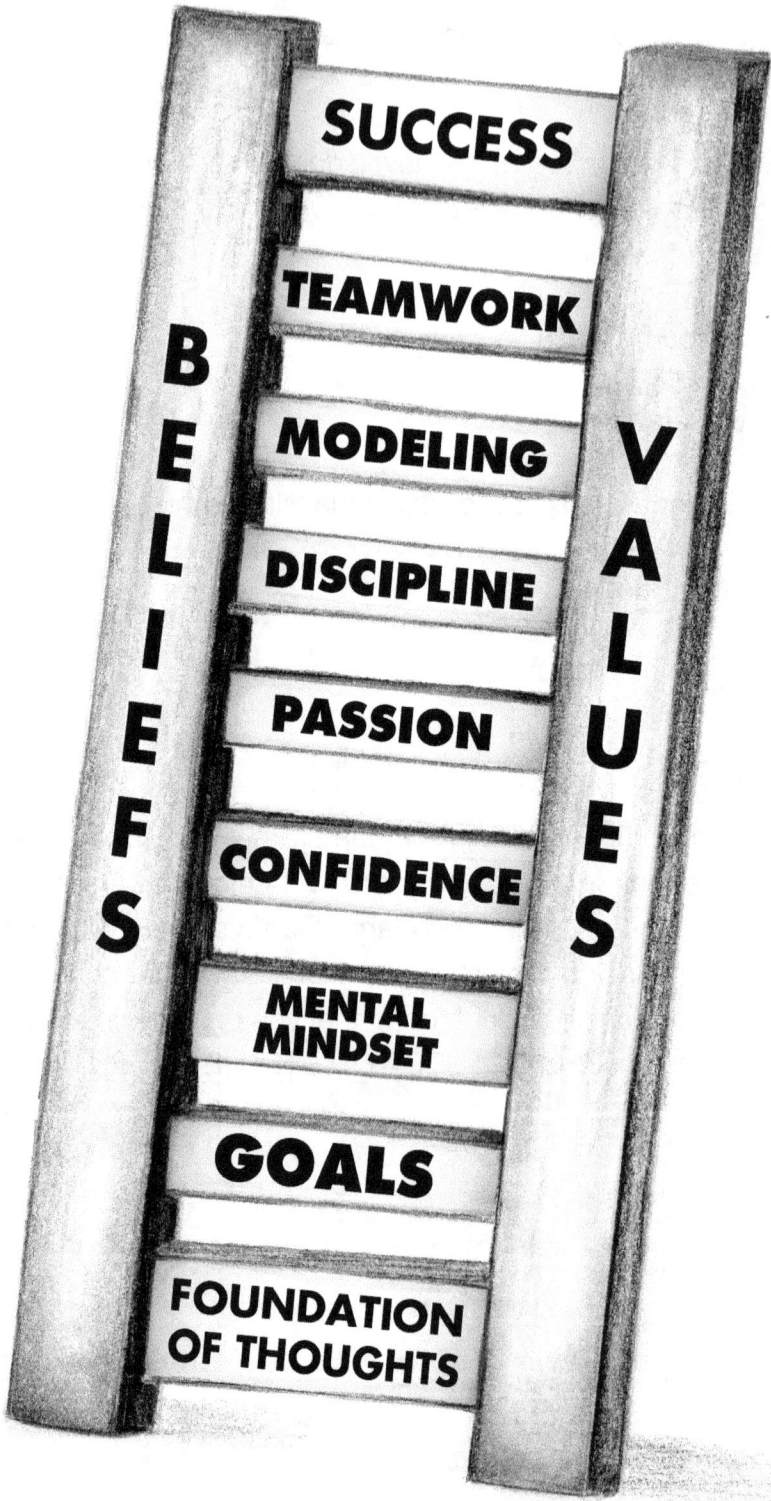

Epilogue:

THE LADDER OF SUCCESS BUILDS CHAMPIONS IN THE GAME OF LIFE

We have now reached the final chapter and it's time to tie it all together. This is like the final day of practice before stepping into your big championship game or match. Have you raised your *Self-Confidence and Mental Mindset?* Is your *Passion* at its highest? Has your *Discipline* shown through with dedication? Is your *Team* ready to go and are you at the stage to accomplish your ultimate *Goal*? Have you found someone to *Model*? All right, so what is left? A Game Plan to put it all together.

Now that you are aware of *The 7 Success Principles for Youth Sports – Goals, Mental Mindset, Confidence, Passion, Discipline, Modeling, and Teamwork –* it's time to set up your Game Plan. Through this book you have been provided the basic success principles of not just professional athletes but professionals in business and many other facets of life. I have attempted to provide you guidance to start on a journey to accomplish your biggest Goals and Dreams. Reach for the stars. Whatever you are looking to achieve and acquire in your life, someone has most likely already accomplished it or something very similar to it. Always remember these words: *"If they can do it, I can do it."* If you are a high school athlete looking to become a starter on your varsity team, or the varsity starter looking to win a state title, the Goal is the same. Give it all that you are capable of, using all the tools and tips provided within this book, and you will be able to achieve more than you could have imagined before reading this book.

It is now time to take what you have learned and put it into **action**. It has to start with making that *decision* to take daily action even if that action is one small step each day. Envision that you are holding a gun and aiming at a bull's eye. All it takes is one small twitch to miss that target. Now look at the reverse of this: It takes only one small correction to put you on target as that bullet comes closer to the bull's eye. Are you taking those small daily actions to keep you on target to achieve your Goals?

All the points in this book have an important message within them. They will help you start with that thought of what you really are looking to do with your life. No matter what it is in life, everything begins with a thought. Thomas Edison had a thought of creating a light bulb. Henry Ford had a thought of building an automobile. What are your thoughts? Are they productive and positive in nature? Don't let anybody take your Goals and Dreams away from you. You can use *laser focus* to develop some simple everyday steps at an early age so that you will develop habits that are everlasting, providing you the backbone to be successful in all that you wish to be, do, and have.

It is now up to you. How badly do you want it? If your Goal is to wear that Super Bowl ring, or to win that Olympic Gold, the time to get started on the path to achieving is NOW! Don't wait another day or even another hour. No matter what level of sports success you are looking to achieve, do it to the best of your ability and don't ever have a thought that you can't do something. "Can't" is a word that you MUST eliminate from your vocabulary. So let's get started!

"If you think you can or you think you can't, you're right"

— Henry Ford

Success is not an accident. It takes hard work and commitment. *The difference between people who produce positive results and those who don't is not a matter of chance, it's a matter of choice.* Those who perform consistent, laser-focused action steps, climbing steadily along the Ladder of Success, are the ones who have an extremely higher chance of reaching their Goals. First, you MUST decide what you want specifically, and second, you MUST decide that you are willing to pay the price to make it happen. Then, pay that price. The rewards will be plentiful but you must pay the price.

If you have gotten this far in this book I have full faith that you CAN and WILL achieve your Dreams and Goals! I believe in you and now it's time for you to believe in yourself! You have what it takes to reach the top of the Ladder of Success and become a champion in the Game of Life.

I leave you with this motivating poem. This poem was an inspiration to me while I was working out daily to step back on that wrestling mat at the age of 50. I used many of the principles covered in this book to prepare for that day, and they got me though that toughest physical and mental sports challenge of my life. I continue to use these principles daily to achieve all that I do. It's now time for me to pass these on for you to use and for you to also be able to share them with others. I urge you to share them with teammates and work these principles together and hold each other accountable. It's my Goal to share these principles with any and all youth so they may learn the importance of these concepts in order to live a rewarding and gratifying life.

Read and reread this poem from Napoleon Hill's book "Think and Grow Rich." Observe the words that have been emphasized, and you will catch the deep meaning the poet had in mind. Somewhere within you, **YOU have the seeds of Greatness**. It's now time to awaken them and make them grow! **YOU CAN DO IT!**

If you *think* you are beaten, you are,
If you *think* you dare not, you don't
If you like to win, but you *think* you can't,
It is almost certain you won't.

If you *think* you'll lose, you're lost
For out of the world we find,
Success begins with a person's will
It's all in the *state of mind.*

If you *think* you are outclassed, you are,
You've got to *think* high to rise.
You've got to be *sure of yourself* before

You can ever win a prize.

Life's battles don't always go

To the stronger or faster man

But sooner or later the one who wins

Is the one WHO THINKS HE CAN!

I sincerely hope that these *7 Success Principles – Goals and Dreams, Mental Mindset, Confidence, Passion, Discipline, Modeling, and Teamwork –* provide the tools to help every youth get motivated to go after their Dreams no matter what they may be.

Champions and Leaders are born every day. Go out and Build Your Destiny!

"If they can do it, YOU can do it."

"Don't ever let anybody tell you you can't do something"

If I can be of any personal assistance, either with one on one coaching, team coaching or one of my programs go to **www.sportswealthinc.com** or please contact me at **jeff@ sportswealthinc.com**. If you would like to receive weekly insights and tips from me, sport professionals and successful business people please enter your contact info on our Sports Wealth website.

If you are a parent or a coach and would like to hear how Sports Wealth can help you with a workshop and or discounted team coaching program please reach out to me personally.

Lastly, if you have found that any of the principles in the book have helped you or someone you know I would love to hear their story. Feel free to email it to me at **jeff@sportswealthinc. com**

"I Aspire to Inspire the Youth of Today for Their Success in the Future."

— Jeff Pierce

Acknowledgements

It has now come time for me to look back on my reasons for writing this book. I sincerely would like to thank many people who have shared with me these principles that I will share further with others through the physical activity of Youth Sports. I must admit, though, that many of the items I will share are not just from my days of playing sports or coaching sports, or have experienced in the business world, but also from what I have read from many others. I will do my best to now acknowledge those whom I have learned so much from to begin this journey of my Goal to *"ASPIRE TO INSPIRE THE YOUTH OF TODAY FOR THEIR SUCCESS IN THE FUTURE."*

First off, I need to thank my stepson Greg for allowing me to help provide him and his friends with guidance as an assistant coach back in the days when he played competitive soccer. Along this same time frame was a gentleman that I learned so much from, Greg's head coach Al LaBarbera. Al has gone on to become both an excellent NCAA coach and a great private coach to many youth in our area. There are many others that both Al and I coached who have left me with some great memories that I looked back to often as I wrote this book.

I also need to thank my son Kyle for all that we have been through in his days of playing multiple sports. From soccer, wrestling, football and lacrosse Kyle has had experiences that have given me some very strong reasons to write this book. And don't let me forget the days of spending countless hours working on race cars, practicing, and driving hundreds of miles to compete at tracks all over the East Coast. Kyle's determination once he strapped himself to any race car he was driving was certainly a driving force for me to give him the best I could. He certainly exhibited many of the principles I explain within this book.

Now to thank the youngest person who gives me the drive to write this book so that I can provide these principles to his friends, teammates, even competitors and any other youth. That is my grandson, Austin. Austin and Kyle may not be aware until they read this, but they have been my inspiration, driving force and teachers in writing this book. Back when Kyle wrestled in junior high was the first time that I really realized why I never excelled on the wrestling mat. It was a small shift that Kyle made in his attitude that made a huge difference in his performance on the mat. Austin also has found and realized that there are small changes that can make some huge differences over time. I love both of you kids for what you have given me. You have helped me learn more about self-improvement and the 1% Rule. Amazing how we adults can learn from youth if we just open our eyes and mind.

I would also like to thank many authors who have written extraordinary books that I have read and would highly recommend to others:

Napoleon Hill "Think and Grow Rich"

T. Harv Eker "Secrets of the Millionaire Mind"

Steven Covey "7 Habits of Highly Effective People"

David J. Schwartz, Ph.D . "The Magic of Thinking Big"

S. Truett Cathy "How Did You Do It, Truett"
"It's Better to Build Boys Than Mend Men"

Robert G. Hagstrom "The Warren Buffet Way"

Paul McKenna "I Can Make You Confident"

Wayne Dyer "Change Your Thoughts Change Your Life"

Most of all I would like to thank two special authors whose many books I've read and whose seminars I've attended. I have done their self-improvement programs. First, Jack Canfield. Jack's "Chicken Soup for the Soul" books provide great insights and motivation in any aspects of one's life. His "Success Principles" book, workshop and programs have provided me with great tools and tips that I have used in my personal life but that I also share with others within this book. All of the above are wonderful learning tools for anyone, and I urge you to do the same as I did and read any or all of them. I have not listed all of the authors I have read but some of the most memorable are shown above.

The second author and my inspiration coach is Anthony "Tony" Robbins. He is the one person I have learned so much from and try to model as best I can. I got my first Tony Robbins program back in the early 1990s and went half-heartedly through it at the time. I then picked it back up about five years ago and I can say that between his program and coaching Austin and his fellow teammates, I was motivated and inspired to get back on a wrestling mat in 2006.

Tony's books "Unlimited Power" and "Awaken the Giant Within" are surely two of the best books I have ever read and I revisit them often for guidance and inspiration. Tony's "Unleash the Power Within" seminar is extremely uplifting and life changing. I urge all to attend this life changing experience. Through Tony Robbins and Cloe Madanes Strategic Intervention Training Program I have witnessed Tony's unbelievable ability to provide the most amazing ways for people to change their lives. He also provides the insights for others along the journey. I can't thank him enough for all he has provided me through his books and programs.

Most recently I would like to thank Dave Austin the founder and CEO of "Extreme Focus" whom I have followed for a few years on internet forums. Fortunately, I was able to meet him at an event about a year ago and have been blessed to now have the opportunity to become one of his Certified Coaches. We take a very simple "12 Step BE A BEAST Process" to light the fire from inside out, rather than letting the outer circumstances control our lives. It is a unique way to "tap into your animal instincts" and achieve "extreme focus" in all you do.

Lastly and most importantly I need to thank my wife, Terry, for all the times she has put up with me through challenges that we have had to overcome and for the times that I have given more to my jobs than I have to my family and her. Through this process I have found that she is my backbone and inspiration. She has allowed me to go after my dreams and provides guidance, even though sometimes I don't like what I hear, along the journey. Terry has shown me the light in so many other things in my life. Her compassion and giving to others is amazing and would be hard for anybody to match.

With her 30-plus years of working with children I have relied on her guidance many times in writing this book. If I can touch half the number of youths that she has already touched I will be forever grateful. I love you, honey.

Thank you again to all the above, and to all my past coaches and teammates through my days of playing sports myself for all that I have learned from you.

"BUILDING CHAMPIONS hits a Grand Slam!"
Greg Reid, Best Selling Author and Filmmaker

"Growing up as a small town boy with big league dreams I had to learn these principles through trial and error…. what an absolute advantage for any athlete to have the map of a Champions already laid out for them through these brilliant steps"
Jason Botts, former *Texas Ranger Major League Baseball Player,* Founder of Jason Botts Peak State

"Building Champions provides a great resource for athletes and business professionals to get to the next level"
David Meltzer, CEO *Sports 1 Marketing,* and author of *Connected to Goodness*

"Not only has Jeff laid out a step by step process to have in order to gain confidence and build character in BUILDING CHAMPIONS but it is also a great workbook as well. With 4 National wrestling Champions among 3 kids partly due to long and short term goals setting as discussed in BUILDING CHAMPIONS"
Bob Craig, Father of three wrestlers

"As an athlete, I train my mind mentally as hard as I train my body physically. The mental preparation one needs in any aspect of life can be the difference between winning and losing. Overcoming challenges and thriving in adverse conditions in sports, teaches important life lessons that help me to be a champion in everything that I do. Use these principles as outlined in Building Champions to succeed in the game of life"
Shane Austin, Arena Football League Quarterback

"After reading BUILDING CHAMPIONS I have come to a conclusion, that this book is one of the best books to provide you with the insights and resources to help you in your athletic game. It will help you as well in your life after sport which is very important plus prepare you for the Game of Life"

> **Coach Warren Nye**, Peak Performance Life Coach, host of Mind Over Sport Podcast

"BUILDING CHAMPIONS explore the power of positive reinforcement as an essential building block in creating a happy fulfilled life. The many examples in this book demonstrate these concepts, teaching us its important. PARENTS, TEACHERS, COACHES – If you are interested in promoting the power of mindset & creating lifelong success for the youth in your lives- this book is a must read."

> **Shannon Barbato,** CPT, Owner of MA Adventure Boot Camp, Fight 4 Fitness

"This book is a gift to our future generations, thereby making it a gift to us all. Jeff's structured approach to success, whether in sports , in life, in business…. Is key to ensuring that his principles are not just him sharing his knowledge, but rather helping the reader to create a game plan for executing and taking the appropriate actions to win. I wish I read this book as a kid, but I'm grateful to have it in my hands as an adult"

> **Betsy Westhafer**, founder of the ActionMaster Network and Extreme Focus Mental Performance Coach

"Success takes action and knowledge. Take action and read this book and gain the knowledge of what it takes to succeed"

Croix Sather, author of "Dream Big Act Big" and run across America celebrity athlete

"BUILDING CHAMPIONS gives youth athletes and adults the tools needed to achieve their goals and dreams. A must read for any young athlete. Read it, use it's timeless principles and you'll go further that you ever thought possible"

Ruben Gonzalaz, 4 time Olympian, author of "The Courage to Succeed, The Inner Game of Success, Fight for Your Dream, and Award Winning Speaker

"This book is a must read for all. The best thing that this book brings to the table is the positive reinforcement for youth. Coaches, trainers, and athletic directors would be helping their school athletes enormously by getting them to read and then discuss this book. This should be the start of a class named Life101"

Al Labarbera, 25+ years as in individual and soccer team training coach & former *NCAA Coach*